T0214994

SpringerBriefs in Computer Science

More information about this series at http://www.springer.com/series/10028

Chen Xu · Aoying Zhou

Quality-aware Scheduling for Key-value Data Stores

Springer

Chen Xu
Institute for Data Science and Engineering
East China Normal University
Shanghai
China

Aoying Zhou
Institute for Data Science and Engineering
East China Normal University
Shanghai
China

ISSN 2191-5768   ISSN 2191-5776 (electronic)
SpringerBriefs in Computer Science
ISBN 978-3-662-47305-4   ISBN 978-3-662-47306-1   (eBook)
DOI 10.1007/978-3-662-47306-1

Library of Congress Control Number: 2015940432

Springer Heidelberg New York Dordrecht London

Printed on acid-free paper

Springer-Verlag GmbH Berlin Heidelberg is part of Springer Science+Business Media
(www.springer.com)

Preface

Key-value stores widely served as data platforms for various web applications, ranging from Facebook social networking based on Cassandra to Amazon online shopping hosted by Dynamo, providing a distributed solution to cloud computing and big data management. In modern web applications, user experience satisfaction determines the applications' success rate. In order to answer web queries quickly, key-value stores generally employ weak consistency model. This model relaxes the data consistency to improve system performance on query response. However, a drawback is that data accessed by users might be stale. Hence, there is an intrinsic trade-off between query latency and data consistency, which has become a key factor in the design of large-scale data management systems.

In particular, data consistency expresses as the freshness of data accessed by queries at a local node. Clearly, the latency/consistency trade-off at node level boils down to finding the trade-off between query latency (i.e., *Quality of Service* (*QoS*)) and data freshness (i.e., *Quality of Data* (*QoD*)). In real application, different web queries or users would have different expectations in terms of QoS and QoD. Hence, how to optimize QoS and QoD by scheduling queries and updates in key-value stores becomes an important research issue.

Our book comprehensively illustrates quality-aware scheduling in key-value stores. In addition, this work provides scheduling strategies and a prototype framework of quality-aware scheduler as well as a demonstration of online applications. The book offers a rich blend of theory and practice. It is suitable for students, researchers, and practitioners interested in distributed systems, NoSQL key-value stores, and scheduling.

Shanghai, China   Chen Xu
April 2015   Aoying Zhou

Acknowledgments

This work is partially supported by the National Natural Science Foundation of China under grant Nos. 61332006 and 61232002, and the National 863 Program under grant No. 2015AA011508. The authors conducted the research at Shanghai Collaborative Innovation Center of Trustworthy Software for Internet of Things (ZF1213). During the process of writing this book, we refer to the scientific researches of many scholars and experts. Hence, we would like to express our heartfelt thanks to them. Over time, we have been accompanied by a number of people who helped to shape the outcome of this book in one way or another. Hereby, we want to take this opportunity to convey our gratitudes.

We thank Fan Xia, Tao Zhu, and A/Prof. Minqi Zhou at East China Normal University for their countless discussions and comments. Meanwhile, we want to thank Dr. Manohar Kaul at Technische Universität Berlin, Prof. Kun Yue at Yunnan University, and the editors at Springer for their valuable feedback to improve the presentation of this book. In particular, part of the research in this book was done during Chen Xu's visiting at The University of Queensland hosted by Prof. Xiaofang Zhou and Dr. Mohamed A. Sharaf. We would like to thank them for their significant collaborations and insights.

Also, we worked with many great colleagues at Institute for Data Science and Engineering, East China Normal University, on a day-to-day basis. Thank you guys for the great work atmosphere, your sense of humor, and for making the frequent long working hours not feel that bad.

Last but not least, we would like to thank our own families for having our back. Thanks for all of your kind understandings and great supports.

Contents

Chapter 1
Introduction

Abstract Key-value stores provide a distributed solution to cloud computing and big data management. Generally, key-value stores employ a weak consistency model, which relaxes the data consistency to improve system performance on query response. However, a drawback is that data accessed by users might be stale. Hence, there is an intrinsic trade-off between query latency and data consistency. At a local node, data consistency is expressed as the freshness of data accessed by queries. Hence, the trade-off at node level boils down to finding a suitable trade-off between query latency (i.e., *quality of service (QoS)*) and data freshness (i.e., *quality of data (QoD)*). This chapter provides an introduction of quality-aware scheduling for key-value stores which balances the aforementioned trade-off. In the following, Sect. 1.1 introduces the application scenarios of quality-aware scheduling for key-value data stores; Sect. 1.2 highlights the significance and challenges of the research in this book; Sect. 1.3 illustrates an implementation framework of this study; Sect. 1.4 provides an overview of this book.

Keywords Motivation · Architecture · Framework · Overview

1.1 Application Scenarios

In modern web applications, user experience satisfaction determines the applications' success rate (and keeps the competitors "more than a click away" [1]). The continuous growth in database-driven web applications as well as the complexity of user requirements requires rethinking the traditional database solutions. It results in a new generation of highly distributed data management platforms. Platforms specifically designed to meet the ever stringent performance requirements expected by today's end users. These new generations of highly distributed data management platforms are usually termed as NoSQL databases which often exhibit the characteristics such as schema-free, easy replication support, simple API, eventually consistent/BASE[1] (not ACID[2]) and a huge amount of data. NoSQL databases are categorized as

---

[1] Basically Available, Soft state, Eventual consistency.
[2] Atomicity, Consistency, Isolation, Durability.

© The Author(s) 2015   1
C. Xu and A. Zhou, *Quality-aware Scheduling for Key-value Data Stores*,
SpringerBriefs in Computer Science, DOI 10.1007/978-3-662-47306-1_1

key-value stores, document store, graph database, and so on. In particular, key-value stores have become quite popular. Examples of such key-value stores include Dynamo [2] at Amazon, PNUTS [3] at Yahoo!, BigTable [4] at Google, Cassandra [5] at Facebook, HBase [6] at Apache, Riak at Basho, and Voldemort [7] at LinkedIn.

Key-value data stores are widely adopted by various web applications, ranging from online shopping to social networking. In order to handle big data, key-value data stores resort to more relaxed design choices, such as not supporting strict transactions, i.e., ACID. For instance, BigTable only supports the transaction on a single row rather than the one on multirow and no serializability of read or write operations on multiple rows. In contrast, conventional relational databases ensure a *serializable* schedule for concurrent transactions. In particular, a transaction schedule is serializable if its outcome (e.g., the resulting database state) is equal to the outcome of its transactions executed serially, i.e., sequentially without overlapping in time. However, achieving serializability for web transactions over a globally replicated and distributed system is very expensive and often unnecessary [3]. On the other hand, key-value stores often adopt weak consistency between several replicas. That is, once a write request returns successfully, the subsequent reads of the object might not see the effect of the write. For instance, Dynamo is designed to be an eventually consistent [2] data store where all updates reach all replicas eventually, so that at any time the data queried might not be recent. Similarly, PNUTS provides a timeline consistency [3] model where all replicas will go through the same sequence of updates. However, data accessed by some queries might be stale.

As illustrated above, in order to improve the performance of web applications, key-value stores relax ACID of transactions and employ a weak consistent model. While providing weaker levels of consistency allows for high availability, this often comes at the expense of sacrificing data freshness such that user queries might access stale data [8]. Hence, there is an intrinsic trade-off between latency and consistency, which has become a key factor in the design of large-scale data management systems [9].

In particular, data consistency can be expressed as the freshness of data accessed by queries at a local node; while accessing stale data is typically accepted by most web applications only if the perceived staleness is bounded within some prespecified staleness tolerance [10]. Clearly, the latency/consistency trade-off at node level further turns on the one between query latency and data freshness. Generally, service level agreement (SLA) is used to specify users' expectation on query response. An example of a simple SLA is a web application guaranteeing that it will provide a response within 300 ms for 99.9 % of its requests for a peak client load of 500 requests per second [2]. Similarly, we further introduce the freshness level agreement (FLA) [11] for specifying the user's expectations for data freshness. Interestingly, the SLA and FLA requirements are often at odds. On the one hand, serving stale data could reduce delays and satisfy the prespecified SLAs requirements but that might come at the expense of violating the prespecified FLAs. On the other hand, updating the requested data before serving it could improve freshness to meet the FLA requirements but it incurs additional delays that might lead to violating the prespecified SLAs. Hence, in this work, *Quality of Service* (QoS) is employed to qualify the satisfaction on user specified SLA; whereas, *quality of data* (QoD) is used to measure the satisfaction on FLA. In real life, different users would have different expectations in terms of QoS and QoD, or even a user would have different requirements on different queries of in terms of QoS and QoD.

Example 1.1 Every time a user logs onto her account on Twitter, she receives the latest tweets generated by her followees in the form of a list that is ordered by recency. This functionality is usually termed as *timeline query*. Supposing Twitter adopts key-value stores like Cassandra as data platform, a tweet (including content, creation time, etc.) is stored in a super column where the tweets generated by the same user are inserted into a single row with the user id as the key. Hence, a timeline query typically involves issuing many read queries to the key-value data store so that to retrieve the latest updates generated by each followee. Intuitively, a microblogging user expects a very short response time to their timeline queries while also expecting to see a list that includes all the recent tweets. However, achieving both tasks simultaneously is usually difficult.

In the context of this work, a short response time and the recent tweets reflects users' expectation on QoS and QoD, respectively. However, microblogging applications typically host hundreds of millions of users and different users would have different expectations in terms of QoS and QoD. In such scenario, providing differentiated service is necessary. This application could allow users to specify their expectations on QoS and QoD so that to try best to meet users' expectations on QoS and QoD by appropriate scheduling for these requests according to users' specifications. Alternatively, this application could set QoS and QoD requirements in advance. For instance, setting high QoS and QoD requirements for VIP users, whereas general users are provided by low QoS and QoD expectations.

Example 1.2 Amazon employs Dynamo as their data platform to support online shopping where the information on a commodity could be organized as a key-value pair. In order to reduce the latency of website response and ensure the availability of services, each data object in Dynamo usually has several replicas. As a global online shopping website, Amazon hosts several data center geographically located in different venues. Hence, commodity information might be stored in one data center or multiple data centers. The data provided by Dynamo API might be stale, since Dynamo system employs eventual consistency. That is, the information for customers might not be the most recent.

As mentioned in [2], an interactive session between a customer and Amazon's navigation page would involves issuing several key-based queries to the Dynamo key-value data store. For example, on the web page illustrated in Fig. 1.1, three different queries could be issued to read the data values corresponding to the following zones (i.e., fragments):

1. *Recommendation list* (zone A): This list provides customers the commodities they might be interested in. The system should display this list as soon as possible, as it entails potential profits. If the recommendation list contains stale information such as rating and review count, it might be acceptable to provide some stale information since customers generally care more about the name and image of

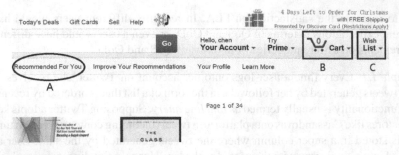

Fig. 1.1 Online shopping Website at Amazon

commodities. Hence, the queries issued by clicking the recommendation list have a high QoS requirement and a low QoD requirement relatively.

2. *Shopping cart* (zone B): Shopping cart stores the commodities that customers intend to purchase but have not ordered. Different from recommendations, all information in the shopping cart list should be fresh and exact. Otherwise, it would bring serious results. However, small delays are acceptable and tolerated, since customers have made a decision to purchase them with more patient. Hence, the queries issued by clicking shopping cart have a low QoS requirement and a high QoD requirement relatively.

3. *Wish list* (zone C): Wish list records the commodities that customers might purchase in the future and they would like to share with their friends. In particular, a customer checking her wish list might tolerate some delays but she is not as committed to wait as someone who has already finished a purchase and waiting for check out. Meanwhile, she also expects to see fresh updates on her wish list items but providing slightly stale items entails no serious consequences (as opposed to purchasing). Hence, it represents moderate expectations in terms of both QoS and QoD.

Therefore, this application could predefine the requirements on QoS and QoD for the aforementioned queries. The system appropriately schedules those queries to meet users' expectations on QoS and QoD as satisfactorily as possible, which would improve users' experiences and increase potential profits.

The above examples clearly show that different users or queries can have different expectations in terms of QoS and QoD, which emphasizes the need for employing quality-aware query scheduling in those emerging NoSQL data stores. Our approach achieves this goal by developing efficient quality-aware schedulers for allocating the necessary resources between the foreground user queries and background system-updates at the data store nodes.

1.2 The Research Significance and Challenges

As in the previous discussion, web applications call for quality-aware scheduling. Hence, employing quality-aware scheduling in key-value stores is very necessary as is illustrated in the following.

1. *Quality-aware scheduling efficiently allocates the limited resources on data nodes to serve the high-level applications.* Recent works (e.g., [8, 12–14]) have addressed consistency/latency trade-off at a global-level (i.e., platform-level), often in the light of CAP Theorem [15] and quorum protocols [16]. While those techniques effectively direct the incoming queries and updates to the right nodes at the right time, it is still crucial to effectively allocate the resources necessary to execute such operations once they have reached their destination nodes where the final data processing stages take place. Hence, the trade-off between latency and consistency is further propagated to each data node and is primarily influenced by the resource scheduling strategy. For instance, Dynamo employs a basic strategy in which replica synchronization tasks are simply executed in the background at low priority, which clearly leads to the negative impact of compromising data freshness [2]. Hence, in this context, quality-aware scheduling is responsible for allocating the limited computational resources at each replica, which would support the high-level applications.
2. *Quality-aware scheduling would account for both QoS and QoD to improve the usability of weak consistent model.* Key-value stores such as Dynamo introduce consistency level as a parameter in their APIs to specify the expectation on data freshness. However, it provides an interface to specify QoS but is oblivious to QoS. RECODS [17] attempts to maximize a replica consistency (i.e., QoD) within some prespecified latency (i.e., QoS) constraint per request, which overlooks the discrepancy between the constraints specified for different requests and their impact on effective resource allocation. DBSoc [18] leverages probabilistic models to analyze the consistency for eventually consistent data stores, but is oblivious to QoS. Differently, quality-aware scheduling accounts for both QoS and QoD comprehensively, so as to improve the usability of weak consistent model.
3. *Quality-aware scheduling would support online applications to improve the user experience of these applications.* For many online applications, different users or queries have different expectations in terms of QoS and QoD. For instance, different users on their timeline queries in Twitter have different expectations on QoS and QoD, and different queries in navigation page of online shopping website have different requirements on QoS and QoD. Queries in key-value stores typically are taken over by the threads in operating system. However, policies such as shortest seek time first (SSTF) and elevator algorithm (SCAN) [19] in operating system is oblivious to high-level requirements on QoS and QoD. It could be compensated by introducing quality-aware scheduling, so as to improve users' experiences for online applications, or even increase the potential commercial profit. Hence, quality-aware scheduling can be adopted widely in web scenarios, which efficiently supports the development of online applications.

In this study, we comprehensively consider both QoS and QoD and provide a suite of quality-aware scheduling strategies to efficiently allocate computational resources which support the development of online applications. In order to achieve that goal, it is indispensable to break down the challenges as follows.

- *First, how to model QoS and QoD as well as their metrics based on key-value stores.* Quality-aware scheduling depends on the metrics of QoS and QoD which should account for the meaning in practice. For one thing, SLA employs response time to qualify QoS. In particular, it adopts a function (e.g., stepwise function [20] and piecewise linear function [21], etc.) on the time difference between finish time and deadline to measure QoS. For another thing, there are many metrics to qualify QoD. Time-based function uses the time elapsed from the previous update to quantify how stale a certain data object is. Lag-based function employs the number of unapplied updates to quantify how stale a certain fragment is. Divergence-based function compares the current version with the most up-to-date version and quantify the difference in values (i.e., the divergence). Hence, in order to appropriately define the quality-aware scheduling problem, it is necessary to model QoS and QoD metrics considering the properties of key-value stores.
- *Then how to design fast, efficient, and general quality-aware strategies for key-value stores.* Different from relational database, key-value stores access the data objects (i.e., key-value pairs) based on key, which is simple and easy to find the updates or queries to access the same data object. On the one hand, quality-aware scheduling should explore this feature to optimize QoS and QoD in the new context of key-value stores. On the other hand, the overhead incurred by scheduling approaches should be sharped in an appropriate range, so as to provide a fast and efficient quality-aware scheduling. In addition, the detail implementations are different from each other for various key-value stores. For example, the value in key-value pair is organized as a blob by the system such as Dynmao; whereas, the one is treated as structured value in the system such as PNUTS, BigTable, and Cassandra. Some key-value stores employ state-transfer model in update propagation and others adopts operation-transfer model. Hence, it is necessary to provide relatively general scheduling strategies so as to adapt to different key-value stores conveniently.
- *Lastly, how to integrate quality-aware scheduler with the key-value stores and flexibly support online applications.* Key-value store is a completed physical system. Before embedding a quality-aware scheduler in key-value store, it is indispensable to have a comprehensive understanding on system; while key-value stores might be implemented in different programming language, we propose to implement the prototype in Java. Hence, this component should be modular and dependent so as to reduce the modification in planting. Meanwhile, it is important to consider the extensibility in implementation, in order to support the version upgrade and maintenance. In addition, the prototype should have the appropriate APIs to flexibly support high-level applications. Hence, integrating quality-aware scheduler with the key-value stores is a critical issue to flexibly support online applications.

In a summary, quality-aware scheduling in key-value stores has both theory value and practical significance.

1.3 Implementation Framework

Figure 1.2 depicts the framework of quality-aware scheduling in key-value stores and also shows the contents of this research. The goal of this framework is: each node in the system efficiently selects and executes the queries or updates from buffer queues in order to maximize users' expectations on QoS and QoD as much as possible, after dispatching the arrival queries and updates. In this work, we formally propose the goal of quality-aware scheduling, design efficient strategies for quality-aware scheduling, implement the prototype of a quality-aware scheduler, and study how to support the typical applications by quality-aware scheduling. In particular, this research includes the following components:

1. *Scheduling objective*: In order to highlight the objective of quality-aware scheduling in key-value stores, we provide the asynchronous update model in distributed key-value stores. At the same time, *quality of service* (QoS) is employed to qualify the satisfaction on user specified SLA; whereas, *quality of data* (QoD) is to measure the satisfaction on FLA. Based on that, we formally define the quality-aware scheduling problem in key-value stores as well as the objective.

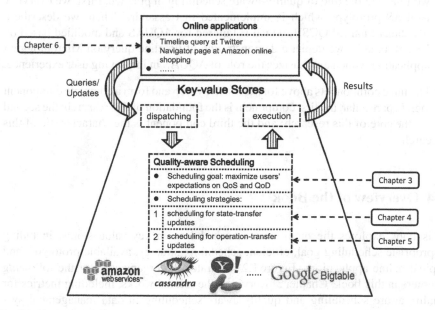

Fig. 1.2 Framework

2. *Scheduling strategy*: Distributed key-value stores asynchronously update several
   replicas of a data object and the updates might be two forms of updates (i.e.,
   state-transfer and operation-transfer updates) according to propagation manners.
   Hence, we study scheduling strategies for these two kinds of updates, respectively.

   - *Scheduling for state-transfer updates*: Under state-transfer update model, the
     propagated updates involve a entire new value. In order to let a replica con-
     verge to recent state, data node simply applies the newest update by skip-
     ping any intermediate ones. Toward the scheduling in key-value data store
     that employs a state-transfer model for update propagation, we propose on-
     demand (OD), hybrid on-demand (HOD), freshness/tardiness (FIT), adaptive
     freshness/tardiness (AFIT) mechanisms and their popularity-aware versions.
   - *Scheduling for operation-transfer updates*: Under operation-transfer update
     model, the propagated updates involve partial content rather than the entire
     value. Hence, each replica basically reconstructs the current value of a data
     object from a history of propagated updates. We extend on-demand (OD),
     hybrid on-demand (HOD), freshness/tardiness (FIT) mechanisms and their
     popularity-aware versions toward the scheduling in key-value data store that
     employs a operation-transfer model for update propagation.

   Hence, we propose scheduling strategies for state-transfer and operation-transfer
   updates, respectively, in order to form a suite of quality-aware scheduling strategies for key-value stores.
3. *Online application*: With the help of prototype as well as the demonstration case,
   we illustrate the role of quality-aware scheduling in practice. First, we overview
   AQUAS prototype which is implemented in Cassandra. Then, we describe a
   benchmark named QCSB, which is tailored for AQUAS and modified based on
   YCSB. Finally, we depict a demonstration of timeline query on Microblogging
   application, which emphasizes the role of AQUAS in improving user experience.

The three components above forward step by step and form a complete component
further. In particular, the first component is the foundation of this research; the second
one is the core of this research; and the third component is the characteristic of this
research.

1.4 Overview of the Book

This book explores the quality-aware scheduling in key-value stores, including
appropriate scheduling goal, efficient scheduling strategy, available prototype, and
typical online applications. Figure 1.2 illustrates the organization of the following
chapters in this book. Chapter 2 overviews the related works, including metrics for
quality-aware scheduling and quality-aware scheduling in data management systems. Chapter 3 studies the properties of key-value stores so as to define the quality-
aware scheduling problem. Quality-aware scheduling strategies for state-transfer

updates and operation-transfer updates are proposed in Chaps. 4 and 5, respectively. In Chap. 6, the theories in previous two chapters are extended into practice by illustrating a prototype of quality-aware scheduler as well as a benchmark named QCSB and a demonstration of timeline query on Microblogging application. Chapter 7 summarizes this book and discusses the future work.

References

1. Sharaf, M.A., Chrysanthis, P.K., Labrinidis, A., Amza, C.: Optimizing i/o-intensive transactions in highly interactive applications. In: SIGMOD Conference, pp. 785–798 (2009)
2. DeCandia, G., Hastorun, D., Jampani, M., Kakulapati, G., Lakshman, A., Pilchin, A., Sivasubramanian, S., Vosshall, P., Vogels, W.: Dynamo: Amazon's highly available key-value store. In: SOSP, pp. 205–220 (2007)
3. Cooper, B.F., Ramakrishnan, R., Srivastava, U., Silberstein, A., Bohannon, P., Jacobsen, H.-A., Puz, N., Weaver, D., Yerneni, R.: Pnuts: Yahoo!'s hosted data serving platform. PVLDB 1(2), 1277–1288 (2008)
4. Chang, F., Dean, J., Ghemawat, S., Hsieh, W.C., Wallach, D.A., Burrows, M., Chandra, T., Fikes, A., Gruber, R.E.: Bigtable: a distributed storage system for structured data. ACM Trans. Comput. Syst. 26(2) (2008)
5. Lakshman, A., Malik, P.: Cassandra: a decentralized structured storage system. Oper. Syst. Rev. 44(2), 35–40 (2010)
6. Apache. Hbase. https://hbase.apache.org
7. LinkedIn. Voldemort. http://www.project-voldemort.com
8. Abadi, D.: Consistency tradeoffs in modern distributed database system design: cap is only part of the story. IEEE Comput. 45(2), 37–42 (2012)
9. Ramakrishnan, R.: Cap and cloud data management. IEEE Comput. 45(2), 43–49 (2012)
10. Guo, H., Larson, P.-Å., Ramakrishnan, R., Goldstein, J.: Relaxed currency and consistency: how to say "good enough" in SQL. In: SIGMOD Conference, pp. 815–826 (2004)
11. Sharaf, M.A., Xu, C., Zhou, X.: Finding the silver lining for data freshness on the cloud: [extended abstract]. In: CloudDB, pp. 49–50 (2012)
12. Bailis, P., Venkataraman, S., Franklin, M.J., Hellerstein, J.M., Stoica, I.: Probabilistically bounded staleness for practical partial quorums. PVLDB 5(8), 776–787 (2012)
13. Golab, W.M., Li, X., Shah, M.A.: Analyzing consistency properties for fun and profit. In: PODC, pp. 197–206 (2011)
14. Wada, H., Fekete, A., Zhao, L., Lee, K., Liu, A.: Data consistency properties and the trade-offs in commercial cloud storage: the consumers' perspective. In: CIDR, pp. 134–143 (2011)
15. Gilbert, S., Lynch, N.A.: Brewer's conjecture and the feasibility of consistent, available, partition-tolerant web services. SIGACT News 33(2), 51–59 (2002)
16. Tanenbaum, A.S., Van Steen, M.: Distributed Systems: Principles and Paradigms. Prentice Hall Inc., Upper Saddle River (2006)
17. Zhu, Y., Yu, P.S., Wang, J.: RECODS: replica consistency-on-demand store. In: ICDE, pp. 1360–1363 (2013)
18. Bailis, P., Venkataraman, S., Franklin, M.J., Hellerstein, J.M., Stoica, I.: PBS at work: advancing data management with consistency metrics. In: SIGMOD Conference, pp. 1113–1116 (2013)
19. Silberschatz, A., Galvin, P.B., Gagne, G., Silberschatz, A.: Operating System Concepts. Addison-Wesley, Reading (1998)
20. Chi, Y., Moon, H.J., Hacigümüs, H., Tatemura, J.: SLA-tree: a framework for efficiently supporting SLA-based decisions in cloud computing. In: EDBT, pp. 129–140 (2011)
21. Chi, Y., Moon, H.J., Hacigümüs, H.: ICBS: incremental cost-based scheduling under piecewise linear SLAs. PVLDB 4(9), 563–574 (2011)

Chapter 2
Literature and Research Review

Abstract Quality-aware scheduling is a novel term employed in our study. However, the related work on this topic appeared in the 1990s. In this chapter, we briefly summarize the literature and research work on quality-aware scheduling. On the one hand, we overview the typical metrics for quality-aware scheduling, including QoS metrics and QoD metrics. On the other hand, we analyze the research progress on quality-aware scheduling in data management systems such as real-time database management system, data stream management system, relational database management system, and key-value data stores. In particular, the goal of quality-aware scheduling includes optimizing QoS, optimizing QoD, as well as optimizing both QoS and QoD. In the following, Sect. 2.1 illustrates metrics for quality-aware scheduling in term of QoS and QoD; Sect. 2.2 describes the research progress on quality-aware scheduling in data management system; Sect. 2.3 summarizes this chapter.

Keywords QoS Metrics · QoD Metrics · Related Work

2.1 Metrics for Quality-Aware Scheduling

How to evaluate the QoS and QoD is a critical issue in the context of quality-aware scheduling. In this section, we briefly overview some metrics for QoS as well as QoD.

2.1.1 QoS Metrics

In the context of data management system, a service-level agreement (SLA) between clients and services engage is a formally negotiated contract where a client and a service agree on several system-related characteristics, which most prominently include the clients expected request rate distribution for a particular API and the expected service latency under those conditions [1]. SLAs are used to indicate the profits the service provider may obtain if the service is delivered at certain levels, and the penalty the service provider has to pay if the agreed-upon performance is not met.

© The Author(s) 2015
C. Xu and A. Zhou, *Quality-aware Scheduling for Key-value Data Stores*,
SpringerBriefs in Computer Science, DOI 10.1007/978-3-662-47306-1_2

Hence, quality of service (QoS) metrics are employed to depict deviations between system behavior and prespecified SLA which evaluates the overall performance of data management systems. There exist many forms of different metrics and we list some of them in the following:

- *Query response time*: The query response time is an intuitive way to measure QoS. In general, the shorter response time is, the more benefit is or the lower cost is. Formally, a function $cost(t)$ is adopted to illustrate the corresponding cost if the response time is t. Typically, $cost(t)$ is a piecewise linear function [2] as the examples shown in Fig. 2.1. In the figure, supposing the query arrives to the system at time 0, the x-axis and y-axis represents query response time t and the cost corresponding to different response time t, respectively. For a number of queries, the total cost is simply summarized as follows:

$$cost = \sum cost(t)$$

- *Deadline miss ratio*: To specify SLA, queries or transactions are usually assigned deadlines. Clearly, queries respond before the deadlines meet the requirements. Otherwise, the requirements are not satisfied. Hence, considering a number of queries, minimizing the number of missed deadlines would improve QoS [3]. Alternatively, the deadline miss ratio is adopted to depict the QoS and defined as

$$MissRate = 100 \times \frac{\#missed}{\#missed + \#met}(\%)$$

where #*missed* and #*met* represent the number of queries that have missed and met their deadlines, respectively.

- *System availability*: Availability is the probability that a system will work as required during the period of a mission. In the context of QoS metrics, availability is based on observations after running a system for a period. Specifically,

$$Availability = 100 \times \frac{T_m}{T_m + T_d}(\%)$$

where T_m is the mission duration and T_d is the observed down time.

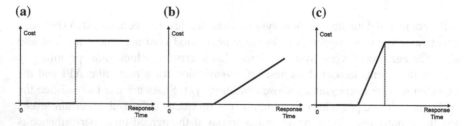

Fig. 2.1 Examples of cost function related to query response time

- *System resources utilization*: The utilization is usually employed to evaluate the utility of each individual node. It is the percentage of the actual running time versus the total running time and formally illustrated as

$$Utilization = 100 \times \frac{T_{total} - T_{idle}}{T_{total}} (\%)$$

where T_{total} is the total running time and T_{idle} is the idle time during system running.
- *System throughput*: The throughput is the number of completed transactions per time unit and the typical time unit is second. Formally, the throughput is specified as

$$Throughput = \frac{\#completedTrans}{T_{total}}$$

where $\#completedTrans$ is the number of completed transactions and T_{total} is total system running time.

The result by metrics above is usually acquired by a long-term observation. In addition to these long-term metrics, transient performance metrics such as overshoot and settling time are adopted for system's responsiveness and efficiency of QoS adaptation.[1]

- *Miss ratio overshoot*: Miss ratio overshoot is the maximum amount that the system overshoots its miss ratio reference divided by its miss ratio reference as

$$M_o = \frac{M_{max} - M_s}{M_s}$$

where M_{max} is the maximun miss ratio and M_s is the desired miss ratio reference. In particular, this reference represents the desired system performance. For example, a particular system may require a deadline miss ratio $M_s = 0$.
- *Utilization overshoot*: Utilization overshoot is the maximum amount that the system overshoots its utilization reference divided by its utilization reference as

$$U_o = \frac{U_{max} - U_s}{U_s}$$

where U_{max} is the maximun utilization and U_s is the desired utilization reference. Similarily, this reference represents the desired system performance. For instance, a particular system may require a CPU utilization $U_s = 90\%$.
- *Settling time*: Settling time takes the system to enter a steady state in response to a load profile. The time represents how fast the system can settle down to steady state with desired miss ratio and/or utilization.

Typically, transient metrics are useful for the performance specification of dynamic systems where performance can be time-varying [5].

---

[1]Reprinted from Ref. [4], with kind permission from Springer Science+Business Media.

2.1.2 QoD Metrics

Quality of data (QoD) is very similar to another terminology, i.e., data quality (DQ). In term of DQ, the data are deemed of high quality if they correctly represent the real-world construct to which they refer. Furthermore, apart from these definitions, as data volume increases, the question of internal consistency within data becomes paramount, regardless of fitness for use for any external purpose, e.g., a person's age and birth date may conflict within different parts of a database [6]. Typically, DQ has a large number of dimensions including accessibility, believability, completeness, reputation, security, etc [7]. However, in the context of quality-aware scheduling, QoD is presented as how "good" the served data are. Goodness of data can be measured in metrics such as freshness that need to be defined from the semantics of the application [8].

In this section, we present an overview of QoD metrics that can be used to measure the freshness of data objects. We present three typical different metrics, i.e., time-base metric, lag-base metric, and divergence-based metric.[2]

- *Time-based metric*: Time-based metric uses the time elapsed from the previous update to quantify how stale a certain data object is. In particular, a function $f(\Delta t)$ is defined to map the time elapsed Δt to another space to describe QoD. For example,

$$f : \Delta t \to [0, 1]$$

is a mapping of the time since last update to a 0–1 range, which is defined similarly to the QoS curves from Aurora [10]. There is an initial period after the last update, for which the value is considered valid and the data item is fresh (and thus the QoD has a value of 1). After this period, the freshness of the data object declines according to a function (which can be linear or any other monotonically decreasing function). The freshness of the data object keeps dropping until 0 and remains 0 after that.

- *Lag-based metric*: Lag-based metric uses the number of unapplied updates to quantify how stale a certain data object is. For instance, the freshness of an object is measured as a decreasing function of the number x of updates missed, and specifically

$$f(x) = a^x \quad x = 0, 1, \ldots$$

where a is defined as the freshness decay rate and has a value between 1 and 0. In semantic, as each object has its own freshness decay rate, a is a knob that can record the varying characteristics of the data objects with regards to freshness or be used to record user preferences. Clearly, there are two special cases, i.e., $a = 1$ and $a = 0$. The value $a = 1$ indicates the user considers the object perfectly fresh no matter how many updates it is lagging; whereas, the value $a = 0$ corresponds to an extremely demanding user who just considers perfectly up-to-date object as

---

[2]Reprinted from Ref. [9], with kind permission from Springer Science+Business Media.

useful one. In particular, the latter is a special case for a binary model [8] where the freshness is 0 if something is stale and 1 if something is fresh.

- *Divergence-based*: Divergence-based metric compares the current version with the most up-to-date version and quantify the difference in values (i.e., the divergence). As the case that data source with stock prices and real-time weather information stored continuously sends updates remote repository [11], the absolute value difference is employed as the divergence metric between a data source S and a data repository P. Suppose x_i^s and x_j^p represent the value of x at S and P, respectively. Let the next update at S be x_{i+1}^s. Thus, the divergence-based value difference between S and P could be presented as

$$|x_j^p - x_{i+1}^s|$$

Instead of absolute difference, normalize the difference (by dividing with the current value) to compute a relative percentage is alternative. Obviously, the relative percentage approach cannot be used in cases where the value domain includes 0.

QoD metrics should be selected according to specific scenarios. Generally, the time-base metrics are especially useful in distributed environments where the exact time of the next update is not known [12]; whereas, lag-based metric metrics are especially useful when we have exact information on the upcoming updates. Divergence-based metrics are especially useful when data object are simple values (e.g., a stock price) but do not work as well on complex data object such as entire web page since it is difficult to accurately quantify the difference between two arbitrary HTML fragments [9].

2.2 Quality-Aware Scheduling in Data Management System

Quality-aware scheduling problem has been studied since 1990s in data management system. These work locates in the context of real-time database management system (RTDBMS), data stream management system (DSMS), and relational database management system (RDBMS), key-value data stores. In the following, we will illustrate quality-aware scheduling in these data management systems.

2.2.1 Quality-Aware Scheduling in RTDBMS

A real-time database management (RTDBMS) is a database system which uses real-time processing to handle workloads whose state is constantly changing. This differs from traditional databases containing persistent data, mostly unaffected by time. For example, a stock market changes very rapidly and is dynamic. Real-time processing means that a transaction is processed fast enough for the result to come back and be acted on right away. RTDBMS is useful for accounting, banking, law, medical records, multimedia, process control, reservation systems, and scientific data analysis [13].

Transaction processing depends on the scheduling strategies adopted by the RTDBMS. To accelerate this processing (i.e., maximize QoS), earliest deadline first (EDF) is used for task scheduling in real-time database. However, it performs bad under heavy workload. Haritsa et al. [3] employs classical EDF to propose AED (adaptive earliest deadline) which aims to reduce the number of missed deadlines. The main idea of AED is to rectify EDF for the context of data access by adding a feedback control mechanism that detects overload conditions so that to modify transaction priority assignments accordingly. In addition, Haritsa et al. [3] also proposes HED (Hierarchical Earliest Deadline), in order to minimize the weighted sum of missed deadlines. It is noticeable that, Buttazzo et al. [14] studies the task scheduling in overloaded context, and argues that EDF is suited for light workload; whereas, SJF (Shortest Job First) performs better than EDF in heavy workload. In general, a real-time database processes various types of tasks (e.g., hash join and external sorting) and it makes sense any deadline misses across the different classes are around a prespecified ratio [15]. Motivated by that, Pang et al. [15] proposes PAQRS (priority adaptation query resource scheduling) which is specifically developed to handle multiclass query workloads in order to minimize the number of missed deadlines. Further, it also ensures that any deadline misses are scattered across the different query classes according to an administratively defined miss distribution.

To improve QoD in RTDBMS influenced by updates, Adelberg et al. [16] discusses several basic strategies on how to apply updates in real-time database systems including: applying updates first, applying updates on demand, split updates, etc. Specifically, the strategy based on applying updates first would install an update whenever it arrives at the system so that all updates have higher priority than queries; whereas, in split updates, updates to important data will be applied on arrival and updates to less important data will be applied when no queries are waiting [16]. Finally, in applying updates on demand, the execution of pending updates is coupled with the arriving of queries, where all the data objects read by a certain query are refreshed on demand before the execution of that query.

In order to guarantee on deadline miss ratio (i.e., maximize QoS) and data freshness (i.e., maximize QoD), Kang et al. [17] proposes QMF (QoS-sensitive approach for Miss ratio and Freshness guarantees) that considers the relationship between updates and queries and utilizes the information to apply the updates required frequently by queries immediately and apply other updates on demand. While that policy considers the dependency between queries and updates, it prioritizes queries based on EDF, which is clearly not an effective policy, especially when system load is high. After that, Kang et al. [18] employs admission controller to improve QMF. When overloaded, update can be relaxed within the specified range of QoD to reduce the update workload if necessary. The modified QMF is just suited for the scenario with firm deadlines, although the performance is improved.

2.2.2 Quality-Aware Scheduling in DSMS

Data stream management system (DSMS) [19] is used to manage continuous data streams and widely adopted in applications such as telecommunication network and finance. It is similar to a database management system (DBMS), which is, however, designed for static data in conventional databases. A DSMS also offers a flexible query processing so that the information needed can be expressed using queries. However, in contrast to a DBMS, a DSMS executes a continuous query that is not only performed once, but also is permanently installed. Therefore, the query is continuously executed until it is explicitly uninstalled. Since most DSMS are data-driven, a continuous query produces new results as long as new data arrive at the system [20].

To reduce query response time (i.e., optimize QoS), Urhan and Franklin [21] proposes the rate-based (RB) policy to schedule a single multistream query with join operators for a query plan in pipeline execution. Sharaf et al. [22, 23] extends RB to schedule multiple continuous queries and proposes HNR (highest normalized rate) so as to reduce the total query response time. In particular, for multiple aggregate continuous queries, Guirguis et al. [24] proposes Weave Share to improve a globe performance by reordering the sequence and sharing partial aggregations. After that, Guirguis et al. [25] employs TriOps to model aggregate continuous queries and proposes TriWeave to further improve the performance on multiple aggregate continuous queries.

To reduce the data staleness (i.e., improve QoD), Golab et al. [26] discusses updating a data warehouse that collects near-real-time data streams from a variety of external sources and proposes EDF-P (Prioritized EDF), MB (Max Benefit) MBL (Max Benefit with Lookahead), etc. The objective is to keep all the tables and materialized views up-to-date as new data arrive over time. Sharaf et al. [27] proposes FAS-MCQ (freshness-aware scheduling of multiple continuous queries) to improve the freshness of results from multiple continuous queries.

In order to balance the trade-off between QoS and QoD, Sharaf et al. improves FAS-MCQ [27] by adding β $(0 \leq \beta \leq 1)$ to propose FAS-MCQ(β) [28]. In particular, FAS-MCQ(β) becomes the original FAS-MCQ when $\beta = 0$, whereas FAS-MCQ(β) behaviors like HNR [22, 23] when $\beta = 1$.

2.2.3 Quality-Aware Scheduling in RDBMS

Relational database management system (RDBMS) is built on the foundation of relational data model and exploits the concepts and techniques on algebra of sets to process data. Relational database is widely adopted in many scenarios. For instance, RDBMS serves as a data platform for various web applications and employed for construction of data warehouse.

Generally, transactions in web applications typically employing SLA to specify QoS are associated with soft deadlines which express the performance expectations of the end user and beyond which transactions are not dropped but are still processed to completion. In this context, minimizing transaction tardiness (i.e., amount of deviation from deadline) rather than the number of miss deadlines is a more appropriate performance goal. As shown in Sect. 2.2.1, EDF is suited for light workload, whereas SJF (shortest job first) performs better than EDF in heavy workload. Sharaf et al. [29] combines EDF with SJF to propose ASETS which is adaptive to the variability of workloads without additional parameters. Guirguis et al. [30] extends ASETS from web transaction level to workflow level including a sequence of web transactions and proposes ASETS* strategy. Sharaf et al. [31] proposes TraQIOS to optimize I/O-intensive transactions in highly interactive applications based on the trade-off between EDF and SJF. In addition, online view materialization is a common approach to process web transaction. Labrinidis and Roussopoulos [9] proposes OVIS(θ) algorithm for the view selection problem, in order to optimize QoS given QoD.

Typically, data replication improves system performance or availability [32]. For instance, data warehouse copies the remote transaction data locally so as to do analysis quickly and web search engine replicates partial web pages to accelerate searching. Hence, how to synchronize the different replicas is very important to optimize QoD. In order to capture users' expectation on QoD, Guo et al. [33] extends SQL by adding C&C constrains which allows users to specify the requirement on data freshness as well as consistency. In addition, Cho and Garcia-Molina [34] studies the update scheduling strategies such as FO (fixed order), RO (random order), and PR (purely random) to maximize the freshness of local replicas. Further, updates influence both the freshness of local replicas and the one of derived data such as materialized views. In addition, Labrinidis and Roussopoulos [8] explores the impact of updates on materialized views and proposes QoDA (QoD-Aware) to find an optimal sequence to refresh materialized view.

To specify users' expectation on query latency and data freshness, Bright and Raschid [35] schedules the transition of web data according to LRP (latency/recency profile). To further specify users' requirement of QoS and QoD, Qu et al. [36] explores USM (user satisfaction metric) to combine users' satisfaction on the query response (i.e., QoS) and data freshness (i.e., QoD) and proposes UNIT framework to manage transaction scheduling. However, USM depicts the QoS and QoD from system aspect and is oblivious to the expectation or preference of individual user. Hence, Labrinidis and Roussopoulos [37] proposes Quality Contracts (QC) which is a framework based on the microeconomic paradigm and provides a very powerful way for users to specify their preferences for query response (QoS) and data freshness (QoD) by specifying how much benefits he/she thinks the server should get at various levels of quality for the posed query. Based on QC model, Qu and Labrinidis [38] proposes a scheme named QUTS (Query Update Time Sharing) that allocates CPU resources to queries and updates based on proportion of QoD and QoS profits assigned by users to maximize total profit.

The classical view of a distributed DBMS is that it should behave just like a centralized DBMS from the point of view of a user; issues arising from distribution of data should be transparent of the user, although, of course, they must be addressed at the implementation level [39]. Hence, it usually employs strong consistency which means that once a write request returns successfully to the client, all subsequent reads of the object—by any client—see the effect of the write. Differently, key-value stores often adopt weak consistency. For instance, Dynamo is designed to be an eventually consistent data store where all updates reach all replicas eventually; whereas, PNUTS provides a timeline consistency model where all replicas will go through the same sequence of updates such that they will eventually converge to the latest update made by the application. Hence, the data provided by API of key-value stores might be stale. For example, if the settings of parameters, i.e., R (read quorum), W (write quorum), and N (the number of replicas), in Dynamo do not meet $R + W > N$, then the result from get() might be stale. When consistency level of get() in Cassandra is set to be ONE, this request would read-any replica of a data object so as to return a stale version. Similarly, Read-any in PNUTS might read a stale data object.

2.2.4 Quality-Aware Scheduling in Key-Value Stores

Similar to the aforementioned data management systems, optimizing QoS and QoD is also very important to key-value stores. In order to optimize QoS, Chi et al. [40] proposes SLA-tree which supports SLA-based scheduling toward benefit optimization in cloud data management system such as key-value stores. Here, SLA is represented as a stepwise function. After that, Chi et al. [2] employs piecewise linear function to describe SLA and provides cost-based iCBS algorithm to support query scheduling in cloud environment. In particular, the cost is evaluated by the mean of the population as the expected running time for a query. However, the execution time distributions might be far from each other. Hence, Chi et al. [41] proposes Shepherd algorithm to exploit distributions of expected running times when doing SLA-aware query scheduling.

In order to improve the performance on query response, key-value stores typically adopt data replication so as to incur data inconsistency potentially which represents as QoD issues at end user. Bailis et al. [42] introduces PBS (probabilistically bounded staleness) to measure the consistency for practical quorum systems such as Dynamo. Then, Bailis et al. [43] illustrates the function of PBS in practice by a microblogging demonstration named DBSoc similar to Twitter. In addition, for weak consistency key-value stores, Zhu et al. [44] studies how to maximize replica consistency (i.e., QoD) within the specified latency (i.e., QoS) constrained by a prototype named RECODS. Golab et al. [45] considers how to detect a consistency violation as soon as it happens as well as quantifying the severity of such violations.

In the context of modern NoSQL key-value data stores, studying the trade-off between latency and consistency has gained special attention and attracted several research efforts. Abadi [46] studies CAP [47] theory in distributed system and rewrites CAP as PACELC. That is, if there is a partition (P), how does the system trade-off availability and consistency (A and C); else (E), when the system is running normally in the absence of partitions, how does the system trade-off

Table 2.1 The design choice of key-value stores under PACELC

System	Partition		Else	
	Availability	Consistency	Latency	Consistency
Dynamo	✓		✓	
Cassandra				
Riak				
BigTable		✓		✓
HBase				
MongoDB	✓			✓
PNUTS		✓	✓	

latency (L) and consistency (C)? Table 2.1 lists the design choices of some key-value stores according to PACELC which emphasizes the importance of the trade-off between latency/consistency(L/C). Ramakrishnan [48] argues that the L/C trade-off has become a key factor in the design of large-scale data management systems. Wada et al. [49] investigates what consumers observe in terms of consistency/latency properties, i.e., the ability to optimize QoS and QoD, under various implementations of key-value data stores such as SimpleDB and S3.

All this work, however, the latency versus consistency trade-off at a global-level is studied and platform-level techniques to model and control such trade-off (e.g., update propagation models, quorum settings, etc.) is employed. While those techniques might be effective in directing the incoming queries and updates to the right nodes at the right time, it is still crucial to efficiently allocate the resources necessary to execute such operations in that final stage in which they have arrived at their destination nodes, especially at times of high load. In particular, it is important that the resource allocation taking place at the node-level works in synergy with the global-level platform design and enforces meeting its expectations and specifications for latency and consistency, which is exactly the focus of the work presented in this paper.

2.3 Summary

In this chapter, we first illustrate the metrics for quality-aware scheduling, including QoS and QoD metrics (Sect. 2.1). Then, we introduce the quality-aware scheduling in data management system (Sect. 2.2), including real-time database management system (Sect. 2.2.1), data stream management system (Sect. 2.2.2), relational database management system (Sect. 2.2.3), and key-value data stores (Sect. 2.2.4). In particular, there are plenty of algorithms, theories, and prototypes with respect to quality-aware scheduling in data management systems. Figure 2.2 depicts them according to the conference or journal published, year, types of data management

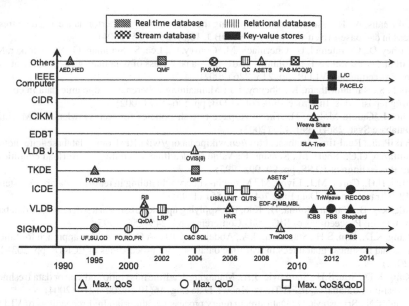

Fig. 2.2 The research progress of quality-aware scheduling in data management systems

systems, and optimization goal. Clearly, there are many papers published on prestigious conferences (e.g., SIGMOD, VLDB, and ICDE) of database community. Hence, quality-aware scheduling is a important issue in data management systems and it calls for further studies for the one in key-value stores.

References

1. DeCandia, G., Hastorun, D., Jampani, M., Kakulapati, G., Lakshman, A., Pilchin, A., Sivasubramanian, S., Vosshall, P., Vogels, W.: Dynamo: Amazon's highly available key-value store. In: Proceedings of SOSP, pp. 205–220 (2007)
2. Chi, Y., Jin Moon, H., Hacigümüs, H.: ICBS: Incremental cost-based scheduling under piecewise linear SLAS. PVLDB **4**(9), 563–574 (2011)
3. Haritsa, J.R., Livny, M., Carey, M.J.: Earliest deadline scheduling for real-time database systems. In: Proceedings of RTSS, pp. 232–242 (1991)
4. Chenyang, L., Stankovic, J.A., Son, S.H., Tao, G.: Feedback control real-time scheduling: framework, modeling, and algorithms. Real-Time Syst. **23**(1), 85–126 (2002)
5. Wei, Y., Son, S.H., Stankovic, J.A., Kang, K.-D.: QoS management in replicated real time databases. In: Proceedings of RTSS, pp. 86–97 (2003)
6. Roebuck, K.: Data Quality: High-Impact Strategies—What You Need to Know: Definitions, Adoptions, Impact, Benefits, Maturity, Vendors. Emereo Pty Limited (2011)
7. Pipino, L., Lee, Y.W., Wang, R.Y.: Data quality assessment. Commun. ACM **45**(4), 211–218 (2002)
8. Labrinidis, A., Roussopoulos, N.: Update propagation strategies for improving the quality of data on the web. In: Proceedings of VLDB, pp. 391–400 (2001)

9. Labrinidis, A., Roussopoulos, N.: Exploring the tradeoff between performance and data freshness in database-driven web servers. VLDB J. **13**(3), 240–255 (2004)
10. Carney, D., Çetintemel, U., Cherniack, M., Convey, C., Lee, S., Seidman, G., Stonebraker, M., Tatbul, N., Zdonik, S.B.: Monitoring streams—a new class of data management applications. In: Proceedings of VLDB, pp. 215–226 (2002)
11. Shah, S., Ramamritham, K., Shenoy, P.J.: Maintaining coherency of dynamic data in cooperating repositories. In: Proceedings of VLDB, pp. 526–537 (2002)
12. Cho, J., Garcia-Molina, H.: Effective page refresh policies for web crawlers. ACM Trans. Database Syst. **28**(4), 390–426 (2003)
13. WikiPedia: Real-time database. http://en.wikipedia.org/wiki/Real-time_database#cite_note-1
14. Buttazzo, G.C., Spuri, M., Sensini, F.: Value vs. deadline scheduling in overload conditions. In: Proceedings of RTSS, pp. 90–99 (1995)
15. Pang, H.H., Carey, M.J., Livny, M.: Multiclass query scheduling in real-time database systems. IEEE Trans. Knowl. Data Eng. **7**(4), 533–551 (1995)
16. Adelberg, B., Garcia-Molina, H., Kao, B.: Applying update streams in a soft real-time database system. In: Proceedings of SIGMOD Conference, pp. 245–256 (1995)
17. Kang, K.D., Son, S.H., Stankovic, J.A., Abdelzaher, T.F.: A QoS-sensitive approach for timeliness and freshness guarantees in real-time databases. In: Proceedings of ECRTS, pp. 203–212 (2002)
18. Kang, K.D., Son, S.H., Stankovic, J.A.: Managing deadline miss ratio and sensor data freshness in real-time databases. IEEE Trans. Knowl. Data Eng. **16**(10), 1200–1216 (2004)
19. Koudas, N., Srivastava, D.: Data stream query processing: atutorial. In: Proceedings of VLDB, p. 1149 (2003)
20. WikiPedia: Data stream management system. http://en.wikipedia.org/wiki/Data_stream_management_system
21. Urhan, T., Franklin, M.J.: Dynamic pipeline scheduling for improving interactive query performance. In: Proceedings of VLDB, pp. 501–510 (2001)
22. Sharaf, M.A., Chrysanthis, P.A., Labrinidis, A., Pruhs, K.: Efficient scheduling of heterogeneous continuous queries. In: Proceedings of VLDB, pp. 511–522 (2006)
23. Sharaf, M.A., Chrysanthis, P.K., Labrinidis, A., Pruhs, K.: Algorithms and metrics for processing multiple heterogeneous continuous queries. ACM Trans. Database Syst. **33**(1), 5 (2008)
24. Guirguis, S., Sharaf, M.A., Chrysanthis, P.A., Labrinidis, A.: Optimized processing of multiple aggregate continuous queries. In: Proceedings of CIKM, pp. 1515–1524 (2011)
25. Guirguis, S., Sharaf, M.A., Chrysanthis, P.K., Labrinidis, A.: Three-level processing of multiple aggregate continuous queries. In: Proceedings of ICDE, pp. 929–940 (2012)
26. Golab, L., Johnson, T., Shkapenyuk, V.: Scheduling updates in a real-time stream warehouse. In: Proceedings of ICDE, pp. 1207–1210 (2009)
27. Sharaf, M.A., Labrinidis, A., Chrysanthis, P.K., Pruhs, K.: Freshness-aware scheduling of continuous queries in the dynamic web. In: Proceedings of WebDB, pp. 73–78 (2005)
28. Sharaf, M.A., Chrysanthis, P.K., Labrinidis, A.: Tuning QoD in stream processing engines. In: Proceedings of ADC, pp. 103–112 (2010)
29. Sharaf, M.A., Guirguis, S., Labrinidis, A., Pruhs, K., Chrysanthis, P.K.: Poster session: ASETS: a self-managing transaction scheduler. In: Proceedings of ICDE Workshops, pp. 56–62 (2008)
30. Guirguis, S., Sharaf, M.A., Chrysanthis, P.K., Labrinidis, A., Pruhs, K.: Adaptive scheduling of web transactions. In: Proceedings of ICDE, pp. 357–368 (2009)
31. Sharaf, M.A., Chrysanthis, P.K., Labrinidis, A., Amza, C.: Optimizing i/o-intensive transactions in highly interactive applications. In: Proceedings of SIGMOD Conference, pp. 785–798 (2009)
32. Gallersdörfer, R., Nicola, M.: Improving performance in replicated databases through relaxed coherency. In: Proceedings of VLDB, pp. 445–456 (1995)
33. Guo, H., Larson, P., Ramakrishnan, R., Goldstein, J.: Relaxed currency and consistency: how to say good enough in SQL. In: Proceedings of SIGMOD Conference, pp. 815–826 (2004)
34. Cho, J., Garcia-Molina, H.: Synchronizing a database to improve freshness. In: Proceedings of SIGMOD Conference, pp. 117–128 (2000)

35. Bright, L., Raschid, L.: Using latency-recency profiles for data delivery on the web. In: Proceedings of VLDB, pp. 550–561 (2002)
36. Qu, H., Labrinidis, A., Mossé, D.: Unit: user-centric transaction management in web-database systems. In: Proceedings of ICDE, p. 33 (2006)
37. Labrinidis, A., Qu, H., Xu, J.: Quality contracts for real-time enterprises. In: Proceedings of BIRTE, pp. 143–156 (2006)
38. Qu, H., Labrinidis, A.: Preference-aware query and update scheduling in web-databases. In: Proceedings of ICDE, pp. 356–365 (2007)
39. Ramakrishnan, R., Gehrke, J.: Database Management Systems. The McGraw-Hill Companies Inc, New York (2003)
40. Chi, Y., Moon, H.J., Hacigümüs, H., Tatemura, J.: SLA-tree: a framework for efficiently supporting SLA-based decisions in cloud computing. In: Proceedings of EDBT, pp. 129–140 (2011)
41. Chi, Y., Hacigümüs, H., Hsiung, W.-P., Naughton, J.F.: Distribution-based query scheduling. PVLDB 6(9), 673–684 (2013)
42. Bailis, P., Venkataraman, S., Franklin, M.J., Hellerstein, J.M., Stoica, I.: Probabilistically bounded staleness for practical partial quorums. PVLDB 5(8), 776–787 (2012)
43. Bailis, P., Venkataraman, S., Franklin, M.J. Hellerstein, J.M., Stoica, I.: PBS at work: advancing data management with consistency metrics. In: Proceedings of SIGMOD Conference, pp. 1113–1116 (2013)
44. Zhu, Y., Yu, P.S., Wang, J.: RECODS: replica consistency-on-demand store. In: Proceedings of ICDE, pp. 1360–1363 (2013)
45. Golab, W.M., Li, X., Shah, M.A.: Analyzing consistency properties for fun and profit. In: Proceedings of PODC, pp. 197–206 (2011)
46. Abadi, D.: Consistency tradeoffs in modern distributed database system design: cap is only part of the story. IEEE Comput. 45(2), 37–42 (2012)
47. Gilbert, S., Lynch, N.A.: Brewer's conjecture and the feasibility of consistent, available, partition-tolerant web services. SIGACT News 33(2), 51–59 (2002)
48. Ramakrishnan, R.: Cap and cloud data management. IEEE Comput. 45(2), 43–49 (2012)
49. Wada, H., Fekete, A., Zhao, L., Lee, K., Liu, A.: Data consistency properties and the tradeoffs in commercial cloud storage: the consumers' perspective. In: Proceedings of CIDR, pp. 134–143 (2011)

Chapter 3
Problem Overview

Abstract How to define the quality-aware scheduling problem in key-value stores is the foundation of studying the scheduling strategies. In this chapter (Part of this chapter are reprinted from Xu et al., Distrib Parallel Databases 32(4):535–581, 2014 [1], with kind permission from Springer Science+Business Media.), with a comprehensive analysis on data organization, data replication, and consistency, user queries as well as system updates, we first model the asynchronous update in distributed key-value stores and highlight the difference between state-transfer and operation-transfer updates. Then, we employ a series of parameters to specify users' expectation on QoS and QoD, and propose tardiness on query and staleness of data to measure the satisfaction of users' requirement on QoS and QoD. Hence, motivated by the idea that penalties are incurred if the system cannot meet user prespecified expectation, we formally define our quality-aware scheduling problem in key-value stores since optimizing QoS and QoD is equivalent to minimizing penalties incurred. In the following, Sect. 3.1 introduces preliminaries about key-value stores and models the data access processing; Sect. 3.2 defines the metrics to qualify QoS and QoD, so as to formally illustrate quality-aware scheduling in key-value stores; Sect. 3.3 summarizes this chapter.

Keywords Data Organization · Data Consistency · System Model · Problem Statement

3.1 Background Knowledge

Modern key-value stores are designed and implemented for large-scale data management. Such data stores are expected to meet strict operational requirements in terms of performance, reliability, and efficiency, and to support continuous growth and scalability [2]. Currently, there are many variants of key-value data stores (e.g., PNUTS [3], Dynamo [2], Cassandra [4], and BigTable [5]). Those variants exhibit a large design space in which some of the design choices are shared by different key-value data stores while others are unique to certain stores. In the rest of this section, we highlight some of those design choices which are strongly related with latency versus consistency trade-off. In this section, we comprehensively analyze the

© The Author(s) 2015
C. Xu and A. Zhou, *Quality-aware Scheduling for Key-value Data Stores*,
SpringerBriefs in Computer Science, DOI 10.1007/978-3-662-47306-1_3

design choices of popular key-value stores such as PNUTS and Dymano, and depict a general model to study quality-aware scheduling in key-value stores.

3.1.1 Data Organization

In a key-value data store, data is organized in tables or tablets of objects in which each object is a simple key-value pair [6]. The common abstraction of the value component could be further classified as [7]:

1. Structureless: This model is based on an opaque blob-like object where an application is responsible for the semantic interpretation of the read and write operations (e.g., Dynamo).
2. Structured: This model is based on a schema-like structure where the value component is divided into columns as in traditional row structures (e.g., PNUTS, Cassandra, and BigTable).

The choice of data model consequently determines the choice of the update propagation model (i.e., state-transfer vs. operation-transfer, as described in Sect. 3.1.4). Hence, in this work, we consider both data models and study their impact on the resource allocation and scheduling problem.

3.1.2 Data Replication and Consistency

In key-value stores, partitioning data across the available storage nodes allows the system to incrementally scale out, where adding capacity becomes as simple as adding new servers. Further, in a large-scale web application, users are scattered across the globe which makes it critical to have data replicas on multiple continents for low-latency access [3]. For instance, Dynamo and Cassandra use a synthesis of well-known techniques for data partitioning using consistent hashing [2] as well as data replication.

In this work, we adopt a *single-master* data replication model similar to the one currently employed by the Yahoo! PNUTS [3], where each data object has one master copy and multiple replicas. In that model, all the write operations on a certain object are directed to its master copy, then later propagated to the replicas. This propagation takes place in a *lazy* or *asynchronous* fashion, where a write is installed at the master first and updates are propagated in the background.

One major advantage of that model is allowing for *timeline consistency* where all replicas will go through the same sequence of updates such that they will eventually converge to the latest update made by the application. However, under that model, a data object read by an application might still be stale unless it is the master copy or it is a replica that has been updated. Given that model, a node can serve as master, slave, or both. In the general case, a node typically stores a set of master objects as well as another set of replica objects. A master object is accessed by foreground read and write requests and it is always fresh. Whereas, a replica object is accessed by either a foreground read request (i.e., user query) or a background refresh request (i.e., system update), as shown in Fig. 3.2. In the rest of this discussion, we will focus on the latter set of objects (i.e., replicas) since accessing these ones leads to a trade-off between performance and freshness, which is the focus of this work. In particular, we assume that a database replica B consists of M data objects $\{O_1, O_2, \ldots, O_M\}$ that are accessed simultaneously by both user queries and system updates. These objects might belong to different applications and they are accessed as described in the next sections.

Example 3.1 As shown in Fig. 3.1, a data object whose key is $k1$ has three copies which are located in node A, B, and C, respectively. In particular, the data object on node A is a master copy and the others are slave copies. When node Y receives a query get(k1), it routes the query to node A, B, and C. Here, the queries from node Y to node A, B, and C are user queries. When node X receives a update put(k1), it forwards the update to node A which stores the master copy of data object with key as $k1$. In particular, node A would install this update in foreground. That is, after installing the update, node A returns a successful identification and sends updates to node B and C which is running in background. Here, the updates from A to B or C rather than the one from X to A are considered as system updates.

Example 3.1 clearly shows the quality-aware scheduling problem studies user queries and system updates which are highlighted by the operations with boxes in Fig. 3.1. From the aspect of the whole system, as shown in Fig. 3.2, a node in key-value store continuously receives the arrival user queries and system updates. In this work, we employ quality-aware scheduling strategies to schedule those user queries and system updates.

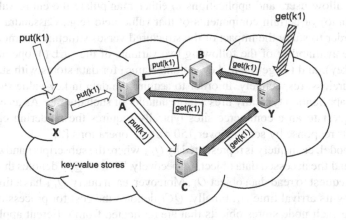

Fig. 3.1 An example of user queries and system updates in key-value stores

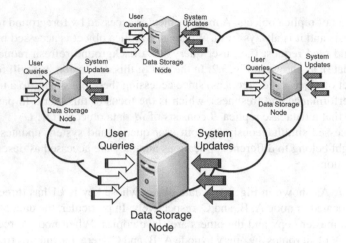

Fig. 3.2 System model. Reprinted from Ref. [1], with kind permission from Springer Science+Business Media

3.1.3 User Queries

Different from the traditional relational database with SQL interface, key-value stores typically provide a simple data access API based on simple methods. For example, Dynamo provides simple `get()` operations for the read and write to a data object that is uniquely identified by a key, while no operation can span multiple data objects. Similarly, PNUTS provides a `get()` operations in a addition to `multiget()` operation which supports retrieving multiple records by specifying a set of primary keys. The particular details of those simple operations depend on several factors including the implemented data model, indexing, etc. In general, however, those operations allow users and applications to either manipulate the entire value field (e.g., Dynamo) or certain components of that value field (e.g., Cassandra). In this work, in order to study the impact of the structured versus structureless models, we assume the availability of the following two variants of the `get()` operation: (1) get(table, key), and (2) get(table, key, columnName) for data stores with structured and structureless, respectively. In order to acquire the data in key-value stores, the high-level application typically fires a large number of such queries. As an example, a page request to an e-commerce sites typically requires the rendering engine to construct its response by sending over 150 `get()` operations [2].

In our model, each query is represented by $Q_{i,k}$ where the subscripts i and k refer to the query and the accessed data object, respectively. That is, $Q_{i,k}$ denotes that the ith query is a request to read data object O_k. Moreover, each query $Q_{i,k}$ has a timestamp representing its arrival time A_i. Finally, QC_k denotes the cost for processing query $Q_{i,k}$. Since each node stores objects that are replicated from different applications and databases, the query processing cost of $Q_{i,k}$ is consequently dependent on the accessed data object O_k and includes the costs for object retrieval (i.e., I/O cost) and processing (i.e., CPU cost). These costs are typically estimated by monitoring the processing of previous queries over a reasonable time window.

3.1.4 System Updates: State-Transfer Versus Operation-Transfer

In addition to provide an interface to get data, key-value stores employ simple APIs for data manipulation. For instance, both put() at Dynamo and set() at PNUTS support the modification on a single row. The high-level applications might modify the data in key-value stores by issuing a serial of set() or put() operations. In the single-master model adopted in this work, after a write operation to an object (i.e., set() or put()) is installed at the master node, it is then propagated asynchronously to all the nodes that store a replica of that object in the form of system updates (as shown in Fig. 3.2). As in general distributed systems, such updates are different from user writes (i.e., transactions) since they are propagated and applied in the background [2]. At each node, the received updates are queued internally in the node's *update queue* until they are scheduled for execution. At this point, it is important to distinguish between two possible forms of updates [8]:

- State-transfer: the master propagates its latest state to the slave, which then replace its current state with the latest state.
- Operation-transfer: the master propagates a sequence of operations to the slave which then applies the operations in its local state.

State-transfer is simple since maintaining consistency only involves sending the new value to other replicas; whereas, operation-transfer is more involved since the client must reconstruct the current value of a replica from a history of propagated updates. However, operation-transfer can be more efficient, especially when the objects are large and operations happen at a high level, such as writes to certain columns in the value like structured data stores. This particular trade-off has motivated us to develop schemes for handling both types of updates as discussed in the next sections.

Meanwhile, for either type of updates, we use $U_{j,k}$ to denotes that the jth update is a request to write data object O_k. Moreover, each update $U_{j,k}$ has a timestamp E_j representing the time when it was generated at the master copy. Finally, each update $U_{j,k}$ is characterized by an update cost, which reflects the time required for processing the update and installing it onto the replica. Similar to queries, this processing time incorporates both CPU and I/O costs. However, the total update cost depends on the form of updates (i.e., State-transfer vs. Operation-transfer). In particular, under state-transfer updates, even if multiple updates are pending for object O_k, only the latest update needs to be installed. In the case of operation-transfer, several updates to object O_k might be applied at once. In either case, we denote the total update cost to object O_k as UC_k, which is easily estimated from recent statistics [9]. In

the following Chapters, we further elaborate on the processing of state-transfer and
operation-transfer updates.

3.2 Problem Statement

The previous section describes the preliminaries of key-value stores. Based on those
preliminaries, in this section, we propose the metrics to capture QoS and QoD, and
formally define the quality-aware scheduling problem in terms of user queries and
system updates. In this work, we focus on metrics that measure success in meeting the
user prespecified requirements. To that end, *service-level agreement (SLA)* has been
widely used to specify the user's expectations and tolerances for response time (i.e.,
delay). Intuitively, SLA acts as a soft deadline where delays beyond the prespecified
SLA incur penalties. In this work, we further introduce the *freshness-level agreement
(FLA)* for specifying QoD in terms of freshness. Similar to SLA, FLA specifies
the user's expectations for staleness in serviced data. Hence, the deviation between
system behavior and user prespecified SLA/FLA reflects QoS/QoD.

To capture these deviations, similar to adopt *C&C* specification in SQL to illustrate user requirement on data consistency [10], a natural way is to specify for each
query $Q_{i,k}$ two deadlines: (1) Tardiness Deadline (TD_i) and (2) Staleness Deadline
(SD_i). In order to fully specify those deadlines and their importances to the user,
each query $Q_{i,k}$ is associated with the following parameters:

- Tardiness Tolerance (γ_i^t): the amount of tardiness tolerated by query $Q_{i,k}$.
- Staleness Tolerance (γ_i^s): the amount of staleness tolerated by query $Q_{i,k}$.
- Weight(w_i): the weight assigned to query $Q_{i,k}$, which represents its importance to
  the system.
- Tardiness Factor $(\alpha_i^t$ or $\alpha_i)$: the fraction of the weight w_i allocated to tardiness,
  which represents the QoS importance to the application.
- Staleness Factor $(\alpha_i^s$ or $1 - \alpha_i)$: the fraction of the weight w_i allocated to
  staleness $(=1.0 - \alpha_i^t)$, which represents the QoD importance to the application.
  Similar to [11] on balancing tardiness and staleness, we suppose $\alpha_i^s = 1 - \alpha_i^t$, or
  alternatively $1 - \alpha_i$.

Clearly, those parameters reflect user expected SLA and FLA. The idea here
to measure QoS and QoD is *if system could not meet user prespecified SLA or
FLA, then penalties are incurred and more penalties mean more deviations between
system behavior and user prespecified SLA or FLA.* In the following, we define
QoS penalty, QoD penalty, and combined penalty, respectively. In particular, QoS
penalty is a common QoS metrics based on query response time and QoD penalty is
a time-based QoD metrics as illustrated in Sect. 2.1.

3.2.1 QoS Penalty

Generally, for a query $Q_{i,k}$, latency L_i represents the time between finish time F_i and arrival time A_i, which is formally defined as:

Definition 3.1 Latency, L_i, for query $Q_{i,k}$ is the total amount of time spent by $Q_{i,k}$ in the system beyond its arrival time A_i. That is, $L_i = F_i - A_i$ since $F_i > A_i$.

For a query $Q_{i,k}$, given its arrival time A_i and tardiness tolerance γ_i^t, the tardiness Deadline (TD_i) for $Q_{i,k}$ is simply computed as:

$$TD_i = A_i + \gamma_i^t \tag{3.1}$$

If $Q_{i,k}$ cannot meet its deadline, the system will still execute it but it will be penalized for the delay beyond the deadline TD_i. This penalty (Fig. 3.3a) per query is known as *tardiness* which is formally defined as:

Definition 3.2 Tardiness, T_i, for query $Q_{i,k}$ is the total amount of time spent by $Q_{i,k}$ in the system beyond its deadline TD_i. That is, $T_i = 0$ if $F_i \leq TD_i$, and $T_i = F_i - TD_i$ otherwise.

Definitions 3.1 and 3.2 show that, latency L_i represents the system performance on query response; whereas, tardiness T_i represents the deviation between system performance and users' expectation on query response. Hence, query should be respond by tardiness deadline ($F_i \leq TD_i$), or equivalently query latency is no more than tardiness tolerance ($L_i \leq \gamma_i^t$), and QoS penalty is incurred otherwise. In particular, QoS penalty considers tardiness T_i, query weight w_i and tardiness factor α_i.

Definition 3.3 QoS penalty for a query $Q_{i,k}$ is a weighted tardiness, i.e., $w_i \alpha_i T_i$.

As shown in Fig. 3.3a, QoS penalty is a piecewise linear function and considered as a piecewise linear SLA. The piecewise linear SLA is simple, however, it is widely adopted in practice to specify users' satisfaction on query response [12–15].

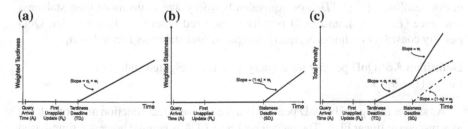

Fig. 3.3 QoS and QoD metrics. **a** Weighted tardiness. **b** Weighted staleness. **c** Total penalty

3.2.2 QoD Penalty

For data object O_k accessed by query $Q_{i,k}$, a parameter R_k is the timestamp of the first unapplied update to O_k. That is, the point in time in which O_k became stale. In particular, if there is no update on O_k, then R_k is set to be positive infinity, i.e., $+\infty$. For a query $Q_{i,k}$, age [16] E_i represents the time between finish time F_i and data stale time R_k, which is formally defined as:

Definition 3.4 Age E_i, for query $Q_{i,k}$ is the total amount of time accumulated by O_k beyond its stale time R_k. That is, $E_i = 0$ if $F_i \le R_k$, and $E_i = F_i - R_k$ otherwise.

Without loss of generality, the staleness tolerance γ_i^s is incorporated to compute the staleness deadline (SD_i) for a query $Q_{i,k}$. Hence, the staleness deadline (SD_i) for $Q_{i,k}$ is simply computed as:

$$SD_i = \begin{cases} R_k + \gamma_i^s & \text{if} R_k \ne +\infty \\ +\infty & \text{otherwise} \end{cases} \tag{3.2}$$

Specifically, at time R_k, data object O_k is rendered stale because of the arrival of a new update that has not been installed yet. If that update is still unapplied until the time $Q_{i,k}$ is scheduled for execution, then the system will still execute the query but it will read stale data and it will be penalized for the amount of staleness beyond the staleness deadline SD_i. Differently, however, in the absence of pending updates, the staleness deadline is infinite. That is, O_k is always fresh at any time $Q_{i,k}$ is to be executed (unless new updates arrive). This penalty (Fig. 3.3b) per query is known as *staleness* which is formally defined as:

Definition 3.5 Staleness, S_i, for query $Q_{i,k}$ is the total amount of staleness accumulated by O_k beyond its staleness deadline SD_i. That is, $S_i = 0$ if $F_i \le SD_i$, and $S_i = F_i - SD_i$ otherwise.

Definitions 3.4 and 3.5 show that, age E_i represents the freshness of data provided by system; whereas, stalness S_i represents the deviation between system behavior and users' expectation on data freshness. Hence, query should be respond by staleness deadline $(F_i \le SD_i)$, or equivalently query age is no more than staleness tolerance $(E_i \le \gamma_i^s)$, and QoD penalty is incurred otherwise. In particular, QoD penalty considers tardiness S_i, query weight w_i and staleness factor $1 - \alpha_i$.

Definition 3.6 QoD penalty for a query $Q_{i,k}$ is a weighted staleness, i.e., $w_i(1 - \alpha_i)S_i$.

As shown in Fig. 3.3b, QoD penalty is a piecewise linear function and considered as a piecewise linear FLA. The piecewise linear FLA is simple; however, time-based piecewise linear function is useful in distributed environment to qualify QoD [17].

3.2.3 Combined Penalty

Based on the above definitions of QoS and QoD penalty, the combined penalty incurred by query $Q_{i,k}$ is computed as follows:

$$P_i = w_i[\alpha_i \times T_i + (1 - \alpha_i) \times S_i] \tag{3.3}$$

where w_i is the weight of query $Q_{i,k}$ and α_i is QoS preference. Hence, $\alpha_i w_i$ is considered as the QoS part of query weight, whereas $(1 - \alpha_i)w_i$ is considered as the QoD part of query weight. As shown in Fig. 3.3a, $\alpha_i w_i T_i$ in Eq. 3.3 is the weighted tardiness, i.e., QoS penalty. As shown in Fig. 3.3b, $(1 - \alpha_i)w_i S_i$ is the weighted staleness, i.e., QoD penalty.

Given N queries in system, our goal is to find a rational executing sequence for those queries in order to minimize the average combined penalty incurred by the system. Hence, the system objective is to minimize the *average combined penalty* which is defined as:

$$P = \frac{1}{N} \sum_{i=1}^{N} P_i \tag{3.4}$$

Table 3.1 lists all the parameters used in this chapter. In particular, γ_i^t, γ_i^s, w_i and α_i could be part of the query interface provided to the end user; or alternatively, they could be set internally by the data management platform so that to enforce competitive

Table 3.1 Parameters in problem statement

Parameter	Symbol
Database	B
Data objects	$\{O_1, \ldots, O_M\}$
Write-only operation: update	$U_{j,k}$
Timestamp of first unapplied update on O_k	R_k
Read-only operation: query	$Q_{i,k}$
Arrival time of query $Q_{i,k}$	A_i
Finish time of query $Q_{i,k}$	F_i
Weight of each query $Q_{i,k}$	w_i
Tardiness factor of query $Q_{i,k}$	α_i^t or α_i
Staleness factor of query $Q_{i,k}$	α_i^s or $1 - \alpha_i$
Tardiness tolerance of query $Q_{i,k}$	γ_i^t
Staleness tolerance of query $Q_{i,k}$	γ_i^s
Tardiness deadline of query $Q_{i,k}$	$TD_i = A_i + \gamma_i^t$
Staleness deadline of query $Q_{i,k}$	$SD_i = R_k + \gamma_i^s$

and differentiated levels of service. Also notice that all of the above parameters are defined from a query perspective and are independent of the characteristics of the object accessed by the query (i.e., O_k). However, those characteristics of the accessed object, together with the query parameters, will shape up the scheduling decision as explained in the following chapters.

3.3 Summary

In this chapter, we first model the distributed key-value stores and focus on the system properties related to quality-aware scheduling (Sect. 3.1). Then, we define QoS penalty and QoD penalty, respectively, and propose the method to compute combined penalty, so that to highlight our objective for quality-aware scheduling (Sect. 3.2).

References

1. Xu, C., Sharaf, M.A., Zhou, X., Zhou, A.: Quality-aware schedulers for weak consistency key-value data stores. Distrib. Parallel Databases **32**(4), 535–581 (2014)
2. DeCandia, G., Hastorun, D., Jampani, M., Kakulapati, G., Lakshman, A., Pilchin, A., Sivasubramanian, S., Vosshall, P., Vogels, W.: Dynamo: Amazon's highly available key-value store. In: SOSP, pp. 205–220 (2007)
3. Cooper, B.F., Ramakrishnan, R., Srivastava, U., Silberstein, A., Bohannon, P., Jacobsen, H., Puz, N., Weaver, D., Yerneni, R.: Pnuts: Yahoo!'s hosted data serving platform. PVLDB **1**(2), 1277–1288 (2008)
4. Lakshman, A., Malik, P.: Cassandra: a decentralized structured storage system. Operat. Syst. Rev. **44**(2), 35–40 (2010)
5. Chang, F., Dean, J., Ghemawat, S., Hsieh, W.C., Wallach, D.A., Burrows, M., Chandra, T., Fikes, A., Gruber, R.E.: Bigtable: a distributed storage system for structured data. ACM Trans. Comput. Syst. **26**(2), 4:1–4:26 (2008)
6. Cattell, Rick: ScalableSQL and NoSQL data stores. SIGMOD Rec. **39**(4), 12–27 (2010)
7. Agrawal, D., El Abbadi, A., Antony, S., Das, S.: Data management challenges in cloud computing infrastructures. In: DNIS, pp. 1–10 (2010)
8. Saito, Y., Shapiro, M.: Optimistic replication. ACM Comput. Surv. **37**(1), 42–81 (2005)
9. Zhu, Y., Yu, P.S., Wang, J.: Records: replica consistency-on-demand store. In: ICDE, pp. 1360–1363 (2013)
10. Guo, H., Larson, P., Ramakrishnan, R., Goldstein, J.: Relaxed currency and consistency: how to say "good enough" in SQL. In: SIGMOD Conference, pp. 815–826 (2004)
11. Bright, L., Raschid, L.: Using latency-recency profiles for data delivery on the web. In: VLDB, pp. 550–561 (2002)
12. Chi, Y., Jin Moon, H., Hacigümüs, H.: ICBS: Incremental cost-based scheduling under piecewise linear SLAs. PVLDB **4**(9), 563–574 (2011)
13. Guirguis, S., Sharaf, M.A., Chrysanthis, P.K.: Alexandros Labrinidis, and Kirk Pruhs. Adaptive scheduling of web transactions. In: ICDE, pp. 357–368 (2009)
14. Zhang, L., Ardagna, D.: SLA based profit optimization in autonomic computing systems. In: ICSOC, pp. 173–182 (2004)

15. Irwin, D.E., Grit, L.E., Chase, J.S.: Balancing risk and reward in a market-based task service. In: HPDC, pp. 160–169 (2004)
16. Bouzeghoub, M., Peralta, V.: A framework for analysis of data freshness. In: IQIS, pp. 59–67 (2004)
17. Labrinidis, A., Roussopoulos, N.: Exploring the tradeoff between performance and data freshness in database-driven web servers. VLDB J. **13**(3), 240–255 (2004)

Chapter 4
Scheduling for State-Transfer Updates

Abstract Under the state-transfer update model, the propagated updates involve an entirely new value. The arrival of a new update to a certain record makes any pending update to that same record worthless. That is, a replica can converge simply by applying the newest update but skipping any intermediate ones. This manner is suited for key-value stores with structureless values which are opaque blob-like objects where an application is responsible for the semantic interpretation of the read and write operations. In particular, each data object in key-value stores is accessed by its key leading to a clear relationship between the arriving queries and their corresponding pending updates. In this chapter (Part of this chapter are reprinted from Xu et al., DASFAA 1:86–100, 2013 [1], Xu et al., Distrib Parallel Databases 32(4):535–581, 2014 [2], with kind permission from Springer Science+Business Media.), based on a state-transfer model for update propagation, we present scheduling strategies for the efficient processing of both pending queries and updates at key-value data store nodes. In the following, Sect. 4.1 illustrates on-demand (OD) mechanism; Sect. 4.2 describes hybrid on-demand (HOD) mechanism; Sect. 4.3 presents freshness/tardiness (FIT) mechanism; Sect. 4.4 introduces adaptive freshness/tardiness (AFIT) mechanism; Sect. 4.5 introduces popularity-aware mechanism; Sect. 4.6 shows the design of simulation platform as well as experimental analysis; Sect. 4.7 summarizes this chapter.

Keywords State-transfer · Scheduling Mechanism · Scheduling Policy · Experiment

4.1 On-Demand (OD) Mechanism

For each of the presented strategies, we follow the popular design principle on the separation of *mechanism* and *policy* [3]. In particular, we make the distinction between the high-level general mechanism used for specifying the dependency between queries and updates as well as their roles in scheduling decisions; whereas the low-level scheduling policy used for ordering the execution of those queries and updates.

© The Author(s) 2015

C. Xu and A. Zhou, *Quality-aware Scheduling for Key-value Data Stores*,
SpringerBriefs in Computer Science, DOI 10.1007/978-3-662-47306-1_4

Algorithm 4.1: Framework for OD/HOD Mechanism

```
1  while true do
2  |   foreach query Q_{i,k} in current query queue do
3  |   |   V_{i,k} ← the priority of Q_{i,k};
4  |   end
5  |   Q_{x,y} ← the query with the highest priority;
6  |   switch update model do
7  |   |   case state-transfer:
8  |   |   |   RefreshStateTransfer(O_y); // call Algorithm 4.2
9  |   |   endsw
10 |   |   case operation-transfer:
11 |   |   |   RefreshOperationTransfer(O_y); // call Algorithm 5.1
12 |   |   endsw
13 |   endsw
14 |   remove Q_{x,y} from query queue;
15 |   execute query Q_{x,y};
16 end
```

Algorithm 4.2: RefreshStateTransfer(O_k)//Refreshing under state-transfer updates

---

Input : data object O_k
Output: new data object O_k
```
1  U_{j,k} ← the most recent update on data object O_k ;
2  O_k ← O_k + U_{j,k}; // refresh data object O_k
3  return O_k ;
```

In this section, we present on-demand (OD) [4] mechanism. This mechanism does not install the arrival updates immediately, but defers refreshing an object until it is requested by a query. Hence, OD mechanism *couples* the execution of the pending replica updates with the arriving user queries. This mechanism is especially attractive for key-value data stores in which each data object is accessed by its key leading to a clear relationship between the arriving queries and their corresponding pending updates. First-come-first-served (FCFS), earliest deadline first (EDF), weight shortest job first (WSJF) and the other polices could work in synergy with OD mechanism.

Further, the OD mechanism also allows for minimizing the system resources needed to install replica updates in a timeline consistency system that implements state-transfer update propagation. To explain this, notice that under the state-transfer update propagation, updates are *blind* operations that do not require reading the current value of a record before updating it. Hence, for the single-master model adopted in our work, all replicas will go through the same sequence of blind updates such that they will eventually converge to the latest update made by the application. Accordingly, the arrival of a new update to a certain record will make any pending update to that same record worthless as in the *Thomas Write Rule* [5]. That is, a replica can converge simply by applying the newest update skipping any intermediate ones. Since OD defers updating an object until it is queried, it allows for saving system resources that otherwise would have been unnecessarily wasted on installing intermediate updates.

Given the advantages of the OD mechanism, we have decided to further investigate its underlying scheduling policies. In general, under OD, queries are always given precedence over updates. However, when a query $Q_{i,k}$ encounters a stale data object O_k, the update queue will first be checked if there is a pending update to O_k. If an update is found, it is applied before executing the query. This provides an attractive property which is maximizing the freshness of data by applying any pending relevant updates first, which results in almost no penalty for data staleness in our system (i.e., 100 % QoD in the absence of "in-flight" updates). However, in terms of QoS, the traditional OD mechanism suffers from a major drawback as it employs a basic *first-come-first-served* (FCFS) as the scheduling policy of choice, in which the arrival time of query $Q_{i,k}$ determines its priority. FCFS has been shown to perform very poor under deadline-based metrics such as tardiness [6], which leads to high QoS penalties that are expected to overweight the gains from improving QoD provided by the OD mechanism. That clear limitation motivates us to study a straightforward extension of the OD mechanism where we simply replace the FCFS policy with the *weight shortest job first* (WSJF) policy, which is known for performing reasonably well under deadline-based metrics [6]. We have also experimented with extending the OD with other low-level scheduling policies (e.g., *earliest deadline first* (EDF) and density [7]).

All the policies mentioned above (i.e., FCFS, WSJF, EDF, and Density) are *priority-based* scheduling policies. In order to implement them under the OD mechanism, for each pending query $Q_{i,k}$ we compute a *priority* $V_{i,k}$ based on some of the properties of $Q_{i,k}$ and its corresponding data object O_k. For the query with the highest priority, we first apply the pending update (if any) to the data object O_k, then execute the query (see Algorithm 4.1). Clearly, the distinction between the different policies we have studied lies in the parameters chosen for priority computation and how that priority is computed. In the following, we show how such priority is computed under the WSJF policy; whereas, the details of other policies (i.e., FCFS, EDF, and Density) are summarized in Sect. 4.6.1.

4.1.1 WSJF-OD

The WJSF scheduling policy is well known for minimizing the weighted tardiness under high system utilization as opposed to other policies including EDF [7]. This makes WSJF especially attractive for web databases and the applications we are considering in this work. WSJF is basically a greedy heuristic that weighs the "benefit" gained from executing a job against the "cost" incurred in its execution [7]. In the context of our work, that benefit is expressed in terms of minimizing the penalty incurred for violating the QoS and QoD requirements. Hence, the higher the penalty, the higher the benefit. However, notice that when computing that benefit under the OD mechanism, we only need to consider the fraction of the query weight pertaining to QoS (i.e., $\alpha_i w_i$); whereas, the QoD fraction of the weight is irrelevant since updates are applied on-demand before query execution leading to a near-zero loss in QoD for all queries. We refer to that combination in which WSJF is used as the underlying scheduling policy for the OD mechanism as WSJF-OD.

Specifically, under WSJF-OD, each query $Q_{i,k}$ is assigned a priority as follows:

$$V_{i,k} = \frac{\alpha_i w_i}{QC_k} \tag{4.1}$$

where $\alpha_i w_i$ is the QoS fraction of the query weight and QC_k is the query processing cost. It is also worth mentioning that under the OD mechanism, the execution order of updates is determined by the execution order of queries. Hence, there is no need for an update scheduling policy and the scheduling decision is solely based on the query characteristics. Also note that during intervals of light load where queries are more sporadic, updates could be scheduled independently. Specifically, if the query queue is empty, the system starts executing updates until a new query arrives. To schedule those updates, we use the basic shortest job first (SJF) policy where each update is assigned a priority as follows:

$$V_{i,k} = \frac{1}{UC_k} \tag{4.2}$$

where UC_k is the cost of the update to refresh data object O_k.

4.2 Hybrid On-Demand (HOD) Mechanism

In the previous section, we have applied two features of the OD mechanism as described in [4], namely:

1. Refreshing any data object before it is accessed by a query; and
2. Scheduling access to those data objects according to the properties of their corresponding pending queries.

The first feature above enforces the OD mechanism where updates are applied whenever an object is accessed leading to fresh data (i.e., 0 % staleness). Meanwhile, the second feature simplifies the scheduling decision by restricting the priority functions to only the query parameters. However, exploiting only the query parameters in the scheduling decision might have a serious negative impact on the system performance and in turn the perceived QoS.

In particular, OD mechanism is oblivious to the properties of updates which are sometimes in conflict with the properties of the corresponding queries. For instance, under WSJF-OD, if a query $Q_{i,k}$ has the lowest processing cost then it might be selected for execution first regardless of the cost of refreshing its requested data object (i.e., O_k). If the cost of installing that update (i.e., UC_k) happened to be very high, then all pending queries will be delayed and accumulating tardiness results in a poor overall system performance.

To avoid such conflict, in this section, we propose a *hybrid on-demand (HOD)* mechanism, which works like the original on-demand but employs scheduling policies that consider the characteristics of updates in addition to those of queries. In the following, we discuss how to incorporate the WSJF policy into our proposed HOD mechanism.

4.2.1 WSJF-HOD

The HOD mechanism works similar to OD, in which each data object is refreshed before it is read. Hence, the negative impact of installing an update is restricted to the QoS perceived by other queries and it has no effect on their perceived QoD. In particular, processing a certain update with cost UC_k leads to delaying the processing of each query in the system by an amount of time equals to UC_k, which might lead to an increase in the overall tardiness. However, it has no impact on the QoD since data objects are always refreshed before they are read.

Hence, to implement WSJF under HOD mechanism, we simply need to extend the WSJF priority function to include the cost of processing an update in addition to that of processing a query. In particular, under WSJF-HOD, each query $Q_{i,k}$ is assigned a priority as follows:

$$V_{i,k} = \frac{\alpha_i w_i}{QC_k + UC_k} \qquad (4.3)$$

where $\alpha_i w_i$ is the QoS fraction of the query weight, QC_k is the cost of processing query $Q_{i,k}$, and UC_k is the cost of refreshing data object O_k by applying its last pending update. Intuitively, compared to WSJF-OD, the priority function for WSJF-HOD considers the negative impact of accessing a certain data object in terms of both the times it takes to read that object as well as the time it takes to refresh it.

4.3 Freshness/Tardiness (FIT) Mechanism

Both OD and HOD mechanisms defer applying an update as much as possible (i.e., until a query request is about to access a stale data object). For blind state-transfer updates, this allows for saving system resources that otherwise would have been unnecessarily wasted on installing intermediate updates. However, it is often the case that applying the most recent update is not that necessary. This occurs under different conditions such as when the staleness of a data object is within a query's tolerance or in the extreme case when a query actually does not assign any weight to the QoD (i.e., $\alpha_i^s = 0$).

Algorithm 4.3: Framework for FIT in State-transfer Update Model

---

```
 1 while true do
 2    foreach query Qᵢ,ₖ in current query queue do
 3       bᵢ,ₖ ← a boolean variable for Qᵢ,ₖ; // whether to install the update
 4       calculate P̂ₛ and P̂ᵢ;
 5       if P̂ₛ ≥ P̂ᵢ then
 6          Vᵢ,ₖ ← (Vᵢ,ₖ)ᴵ;
 7          bᵢ,ₖ ← true; // install the update
 8       else
 9          Vᵢ,ₖ ← (Vᵢ,ₖ)ˢ;
10          bᵢ,ₖ ← false; // skip the update
11       end
12    end
13    Qₓ,ᵧ ← the query with the highest priority;
14    Oᵧ ← the data object accessed by query Qᵢ,ₖ;
15    if bₓ,ᵧ then
16       RefreshStateTransfer(Oᵧ); // call Algorithm 4.2
17    end
18    remove Qₓ,ᵧ from the query queue;
19    execute Qₓ,ᵧ;
20 end
```

However, even when the staleness of a data object violates the QoD requirements of a certain query, applying a pending update to that object might often be at odds with the processing of user queries. In particular, installing a pending update with a high-processing cost could potentially have the negative impact of delaying all pending user queries leading to an overall low QoS (i.e., high tardiness), despite of the high QoD (i.e., high freshness). Motivated by this observation, we propose the new *freshness/tardiness (FIT)* mechanism for the scheduling of both queries and updates.

FIT, like OD and HOD, defers refreshing an object until it is requested by a query. However, under FIT, the scheduling policy reasons about the global impact of applying an update in terms of the benefits of processing that update to the query under consideration as well as the other queries in the system. In particular, given a query $Q_{i,k}$, the FIT scheduler needs to make two main decisions:

1. Whether the latest pending update to data object O_k (i.e., $U_{j,k}$) is to be skipped or installed?; and
2. How to assign an appropriate priority to each query so that to minimize the overall system penalty?

In order to make the first decision (i.e., whether to skip or install an update $U_{j,k}$), we simply need to compare the approximate total penalty incurred by query $Q_{i,k}$ in each of the following cases:

Skipping update $U_{j,k}$: The total expected penalty $\hat{P}_S$ incurred by $Q_{i,k}$ when $U_{j,k}$ is skipped equals to:

$$\hat{P}_S = (\tau + QC_k - TD_i)^+ \alpha_i w_i + (\tau + QC_k - SD_i)^+ (1 - \alpha_i) w_i \qquad (4.4)$$

where τ is the current system time and QC_k is the cost for processing query $Q_{i,k}$. Thus, $\tau + QC_k$ is the query finish time and $(\tau + QC_k - TD_i)^+$ is basically the equivalent of $max(0, (\tau + QC_k - TD_i))$. That is, only positive tardiness contributes to the penalty. Hence, the first term above represents the tardiness penalty (i.e., $(\tau + QC_k - TD_i)^+ \alpha_i w_i$), whereas the second term represents the staleness penalty (i.e., $(\tau + QC_k - SD_i)^+ (1 - \alpha_i) w_i$).

Installing update $U_{j,k}$: The total expected penalty $\hat{P}_I$ incurred by $Q_{i,k}$ when $U_{j,k}$ is installed equals to

$$\hat{P}_I = (\tau + QC_k + UC_k - TD_i)^+ \alpha_i w_i \qquad (4.5)$$

where the definition of each term is similar to the previous equation. Accordingly, the equation represents the tardiness penalty, whereas the staleness is almost zero since $U_{j,k}$ is applied before answering $Q_{i,k}$ leading to a fresh data object O_k.

Finally, we compare the two values above (i.e., $\hat{P}_S$ and $\hat{P}_I$) to decide whether $U_{j,k}$ should be skipped or installed.

- $\hat{P}_S \geq \hat{P}_I$: indicates that the total penalty incurred by skipping $U_{j,k}$ is more than or equal to that incurred by applying it. Therefore, $U_{j,k}$ should be applied before executing $Q_{i,k}$.
- $\hat{P}_S < \hat{P}_I$: indicates that the total penalty incurred by skipping $U_{j,k}$ is less than that incurred by applying it. Therefore, $Q_{i,k}$ is executed directly and $U_{j,k}$ is skipped.

So far, we have addressed the first decision listed above. This is a *local* decision where for each pending query $Q_{i,k}$, the scheduler has to first decide on the need for refreshing data object O_k before executing $Q_{i,k}$. However, that decision is not actioned until query $Q_{i,k}$ is scheduled for execution. The execution order of query $Q_{i,k}$ is determined by a *global* scheduler that addresses the second decision listed above and is discussed next.

In order to make the global decision under the FIT mechanism, query $Q_{i,k}$ is assigned a priority $V_{i,k}$ which is given one of two possible values according to the outcome of the local decision. As shown in Algorithm 4.3, $V_{i,k}$ is set to be the value $(V_{i,k})^I$ if $Q_{i,k}$ is to be executed together with the latest corresponding update (if any) (line 7), whereas $V_{i,k}$ is equal to $(V_{i,k})^S$ if the update is skipped (line 10). Finally, the query with the highest $V_{i,k}$ is selected for execution and its corresponding update is handled according to the local decision (line 13–19).

In order to understand the computation of $V_{i,k}$, notice that $(V_{i,k})^I$ corresponds to only a QoS penalty as represented in Fig. 3.3a; whereas, $(V_{i,k})^S$ corresponds to a combined QoS and QoD penalty as represented in Fig. 3.3c. Hence, the $(V_{i,k})^I$ priority under FIT is the same as its counterpart under the hybrid on-demand mechanism; whereas, the $(V_{i,k})^S$ priority should reflect the impact of skipping an update.

To compute $(V_{i,k})^S$, we need to consider the impact of an update on both QoS and QoD. From Fig. 3.3c, we notice that the combined penalty is a function in time with

Fig. 4.1 General penalty
function under FIT.
Reprinted from Ref. [2], with
kind permission from
Springer Science+Business
Media

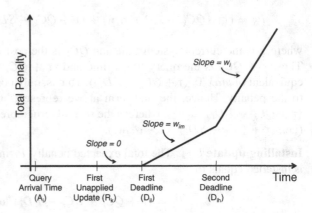

two *critical* points: (1) tardiness deadline and (2) staleness deadline. In particular,
assume the case in Fig. 3.3c where $TD_i < SD_i$, then the penalty is zero up to time
$\tau = TD_i$ then it increases linearly with slope $\alpha_i \times w_i$ reflecting the penalty incurred
by the system for not meeting the tardiness deadline. This slope stays the same until
time $\tau = SD_i$ where the slope increases to be w_i reflecting the combined penalty for
both staleness and tardiness. This slope remains constant until the query is eventually
answered. In the opposite case where $TD_i > SD_i$, the penalty function will have
the same general shape except that the first slope will be $(1 - \alpha_i) \times w_i$.

Given the observations above, we can represent the penalty as a function with two
deadlines (Fig. 4.1), i.e., D_{il} and D_{ih}, and three segments with slopes that have the
following values: (i) 0, if $\tau \leq D_{il}$, (ii) w_{im}, if $D_{il} < \tau \leq D_{ih}$, and (iii) w_i, if $\tau > D_{ih}$.
Such that w_i is the weight when a query misses both its deadline, whereas w_{im} is the
intermediate weight when the query misses one of its deadlines but not both. As such,
if $TD_i < SD_i$, then $w_{im} = \alpha_i \times w_i$ and if $TD_i > SD_i$, then $w_{im} = (1 - \alpha_i) \times w_i$.
Next, we propose WSJF-FIT, the WSJF policy that works in synergy with the FIT
mechanism.

4.3.1 WSJF-FIT

As explained above, under WSJF-FIT, $(V_{i,k})^I$ is computed similar to its hybrid
on-demand counterpart (i.e., WSJF-HOD); whereas, $(V_{i,k})^S$ is computed based on
Fig. 4.1. In particular, $(V_{i,k})^I$ and $(V_{i,k})^S$ are computed as follows:

$$(V_{i,k})^I = \frac{\alpha_i w_i}{QC_k + UC_k}, \quad (V_{i,k})^S = \begin{cases} \frac{w_{im}}{QC_k} & \tau \leq D_{il} \\ \frac{w_i}{QC_k} & \tau > D_{il} \end{cases} \quad (4.6)$$

For $(V_{i,k})^S$ to capture the loss in both QoS and QoD, we simply extended the basic
WSJF policy to consider two deadlines (Fig. 4.1) instead of one deadline (Fig. 3.3a).
To do that, notice that the original WSJF sets the weight parameter according to the

slope of the next *critical point*. Hence, under WSJF-OD and WSJF-HOD, at any time τ, the weight will only have one single value because there is only one critical point. However, under WSJF-FIT, after crossing the first critical point (i.e., D_{il}), the weight would be updated to reflect the future penalty incurred by the system if the query were to be delayed further. In such case, the penalty is expressed by the slope at the next critical point (i.e., D_{ih}).

By considering the query cost QC_k in $(V_{i,k})^S$, WSJF-FIT, like WSJF-HOD, captures the negative impact of running a certain query $Q_{i,k}$ on the other pending queries on the node. Similarly, it also captures the system loss in QoS if $Q_{i,k}$ were to miss its tardiness deadline, which is expressed by the QoS portion of the query weight. But in addition to that, it also captures the system loss in QoD if $Q_{i,k}$ were to access a stale data object, which is expressed by the QoD portion of the query weight.

4.4 Adaptive Freshness/Tardiness (AFIT) Mechanism

The previous OD, HOD, and FIT mechanisms are well suited to optimize resource allocation in key-value data stores so that to maximize both QoS and QoD. However, OD and HOD might sacrifice QoS in order to maximize QoD since it always refreshes a data objects before it is accessed by a query. Although FIT allows to selectively skip some of the pending updates to balance QoS and QoD, it only accounts for the cost of query and update. Further, WSJF-FIT employs a scheduling policy that is purely based on the classical shortest job first (SJF) which is oblivious to deadlines. In general queueing systems, it is well known that earliest deadline first (EDF) works reasonably well in the presence of SLAs except for systems that exhibit high utilization or fairly tight SLAs, in which case SJF typically outperforms EDF [6]. This exact trade-off between EDF and SJF motivates us to further study the performance of query scheduling policies in key-value data stores. In particular, in this work we propose *adaptive freshness/tardiness (AFIT)* an adaptive mechanism for the scheduling of queries and updates in a key-value data store. Like FIT, AFIT employs a selective decision in applying pending updates so that to balance the trade-off between QoS and QoD, and in turn minimize the overall system penalty. Differently, however, AFIT employs a hybrid scheduler that integrates and extends both SJF and EDF into the scheduling decision so that to dynamically adapt to the variability in the workload settings. Following the separation between mechanisms and policies, we propose a new WSJF-AFIT strategy, i.e., WSJF policy that works in synergy with the AFIT mechanism.

As shown in Fig. 4.2, the AFIT mechanism maintains two query lists: (1) *Apply List (AL)*; and (2) *Skip List (SL)*. In both lists, each query is assigned a priority value according to a weighted variant of SJF which considers the trade-off between benefit and cost. As illustrated in Sect. 4.1.1, the benefit is expressed in terms of minimizing the penalty paid by the system for violating the QoS and QoD requirements. Hence, the higher the penalty, the higher the weight (i.e., priority). Accordingly, those priorities are computed as follows:

Fig. 4.2 Framework of
AFIT scheduler

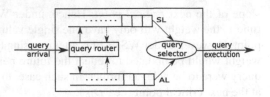

- *Apply List (AL)*: A query $Q_{i,k}$ is added to this list when AFIT decides to apply the latest pending update to the data object accessed by $Q_{i,k}$ before it is executed. Accordingly, each query in this list would access a fresh data object. Hence, AFIT needs to only consider the fraction of weight pertaining to QoS (i.e., α_i) and the priority of each query $Q_{i,k}$ in AL is computed as $V_{i,k} = \frac{\alpha_i w_i}{QC_k + UC_k}$.
- *Skip List (SL)*: A query $Q_{i,k}$ is added to this list when AFIT decides to skip the latest pending update to the data object accessed by $Q_{i,k}$ before it is executed. Accordingly, a query in this list might access a stale data object. Hence, AFIT needs to consider the total weight of QoS and QoD (i.e., w_i) and the priority of each query $Q_{i,k}$ in SL is computed as $V_{i,k} = \frac{w_i}{QC_k}$.

AFIT employs two components, including a query router and a query selector. In Sect. 4.4.1, the query router decides the placement of a new query according to the critical condition described in section. In addition, the query router also checks the existing queries in the two lists and reallocates the queries for which that critical condition has been violated. In Sect. 4.4.2, the query selector component decides the query to be scheduled for execution. The query selector chooses between the two queries with the highest priority in the AL and SL lists and its decision is based on an integration of the SJF and EDF policies. In Sect. 4.4.3, we describe the implementation of WSJF-AFIT-based on the process of query routing and selection.

4.4.1 Query Routing

The query routing component of AFIT is responsible for assigning each newly arriving query to either the AL or the SL list. Central to that decision is estimating the *slack* available for each query. That estimation is dependent on the candidate target list (i.e., AL or SL) as well as the performance metrics under consideration (i.e., tardiness and staleness). Before further discussing the details of query routing, the different definitions of slack are given below:

Definition 4.1 The **AL tardiness slack** time ts_i^a of query $Q_{i,k}$ is the maximum amount of time that $Q_{i,k}$ can wait before it misses its tardiness deadline TD_i. This excludes the cost for applying the last pending update to the accessed data object (i.e., UC_k) and the cost for query execution (i.e., QC_k). Specifically, $ts_i^a = TD_i - (t + QC_k + UC_k)$ where t is the current system time.

Definition 4.2 The **SL tardiness slack** time ts_i^s of query $Q_{i,k}$ is the maximum amount of time that $Q_{i,k}$ can wait before it misses its tardiness deadline TD_i. This excludes the cost for query execution (i.e., QC_k). Specifically, $ts_i^s = TD_i - (t + QC_k)$ where t is the current system time.

Clearly, for any query $Q_{i,k}$, $ts_i^s \geq ts_i^a$ at any time t. That is, the available slack time to meet the tardiness deadline by skipping an update (i.e., ts_i^s) is always greater than or equal the available slack time when an update is to be applied (i.e., ts_i^a). However, if an update is to be skipped, it is essential to measure the available time to meet the staleness deadline. That is, the accessed data object meets the prespecified staleness tolerance, which is defined as

Definition 4.3 The **staleness slack** time ss_i of query $Q_{i,k}$ is the maximum amount of time that $Q_{i,k}$ can wait before it misses its staleness deadline SD_i. This excludes the cost for query execution (i.e., QC_k). Specifically, $ss_i = SD_i - (t + QC_k)$ where t is the current system time.

Intuitively, a query $Q_{i,k}$ is inserted into AL if the penalty incurred by applying the latest pending update is greater than the one incurred by skipping it, and vice versa. Based on the definitions above, the critical condition employed by the query router is represented as *query $Q_{i,k}$ is inserted into AL, if either* Eq. 4.7a, b *meets.*

$$\begin{cases} ts_i^a \geq 0 & \text{a} \\ \alpha_i [UC_k - max(0, ts_i^s)] \leq (1 - \alpha_i) max(0, -ss_i) & \text{b} \end{cases} \tag{4.7}$$

Otherwise, $Q_{i,k}$ would be inserted into SL.

The equations above basically exploit the estimated potential penalty so that to choose the appropriate list assignment for each incoming query. Only a QoS penalty is incurred if the pending update is applied, whereas both QoS and QoD penalties are expected if that update is skipped.

To further explain the intuition underlying the AFIT query router, lets consider the different valid relationships between ts_i^a and ts_i^s as shown in Fig. 4.3a–c.

1. $0 \leq ts_i^a < ts_i^s$: Fig. 4.3a shows that even if $Q_{i,k}$ waits for data refreshing, i.e., no QoD penalty, it still meets its tardiness deadline, i.e. no QoS penalty. Hence, $Q_{i,k}$ should be inserted into AL since Eq. 4.7a is satisfied in that case.
2. $ts_i^a < ts_i^s < 0$: Fig. 4.3b shows the case in which $Q_{i,k}$ will miss its tardiness deadline TD_i, even if the pending update is skipped. Specifically, if the pending update is skipped, $Q_{i,k}$ misses TD_i by $t + QC_k - TD_i$ and misses SD_i by $max(0, t + QC_k - SD_i)$, i.e., $max(0, -ss_i)$. Hence, the total incurred penalty P_s is $\alpha_i w_i (t + QC_k - TD_i) + (1 - \alpha_i) w_i max(0, -ss_i)$. To the contrary, if $Q_{i,k}$ waits for the accessed data object to be updated, the total penalty P_a will only include the QoS component and is estimated as $\alpha_i w_i (t + QC_k + UC_k - TD_i)$. Therefore, $Q_{i,k}$ should be inserted into AL if $P_a \leq P_s$, i.e.,

$$\alpha_i UC_k \leq (1 - \alpha_i) max(0, -ss_i) \tag{4.8}$$

Fig. 4.3 Potential tardiness increased. **a** $0 \leq ts_i^a < ts_i^s$. **b** $ts_i^a < ts_i^s < 0$. **c** $ts_i^a < 0 < ts_i^s$

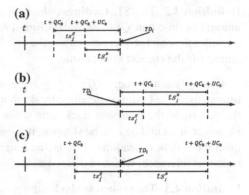

3. $ts_i^a < 0 < ts_i^s$: Fig. 4.3c shows the final case in which $Q_{i,k}$ misses its tardiness deadline TD_i if the data object is refreshed, whereas it meets TD_i if the data object is left stale. Similar to previous case, we compare the penalty incurred by applying or skipping the pending update. If $Q_{i,k}$ skips the update, only QoD penalty is incurred and then the total penalty P_s equals to $(1 - \alpha_i)w_i max(0, -ss_i)$. To the contrary, if $Q_{i,k}$ applies the update, only QoS penalty exists and the total penalty P_a is $\alpha_i w_i (t + QC_k + UC_k - TD_i) = \alpha_i w_i (UC_k - ts_i^s)$. Hence, $Q_{i,k}$ is inserted into AL if $P_a \leq P_s$, i.e.,

$$\alpha_i (UC_k - ts_i^s) \leq (1 - \alpha_i) max(0, -ss_i) \qquad (4.9)$$

In the AFIT query router, the first case above is handled by Eq. 4.7a, whereas the second and third cases are uniformly handled by Eq. 4.7b. In particular, a newly arriving query is dispatched to either AL or SL according to those two equations. Moreover, at each scheduling point, the query router maintains the two lists as follows: (1) queries in SL that satisfy Eq. 4.7a, b are moved into AL; and (2) queries in AL that satisfy neither Eq. 4.7a, b are moved into SL.

4.4.2 Query Selection

Clearly, the query with the highest priority in AL should be executed prior to the other queries in that list. Similarly, the query with the highest priority in SL should be the first one to be executed in that list. Hence, at each scheduling point, the task of the query selector is to compare the head query in AL (say Q_{A1}) to the head query in SL (say Q_{S1}) and the winner is selected for execution (as illustrated in Fig. 4.2).

One option is to compare those two queries according to the weighted SJF priority p_i assigned to them when first inserted in AL and SL, respectively. This is similar to the approach followed by FIT [8], which is purely based on cost-benefit analysis and has the drawback of ignoring the respective deadlines of those two queries. To illustrate the impact of that drawback, consider the following example:

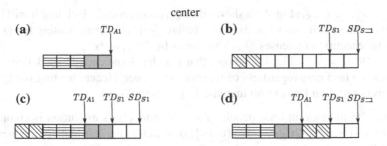

Fig. 4.4 Motivated example for query selection. **a** Q_{A1}: $QC_{A1} = 2$, $UC_{A1} = 3$. **b** Q_{S1}: $QC_{S1} = 2$, $U_{S1} = 6$. **c** Q_{S1} followed by Q_{A1}. **d** Q_{A1} followed by Q_{S1}

Example 4.1 Figure 4.4 shows two queries Q_{A1} and Q_{S1}, for which we assume equal QoS fractions for the two queries (i.e., $\alpha_{A1} = \alpha_{S1}$) as well as equal weights (i.e., $w_{A1} = w_{S1}$). Computing the priority of each query according to weighted SJF results in $V_{A1} = \frac{\alpha_{A1}w_{A1}}{QC_{A1}+UC_{A1}}$ and $V_{S1} = \frac{w_{S1}}{QC_{S1}}$. Given the query and update costs illustrated in Fig. 4.4, in this example $V_{S1} > V_{A1}$ and a simple cost-benefit comparison would result in Q_{S1} being executed before Q_{A1}. However, that exact execution order results in a system penalty (as shown in Fig. 4.4c), whereas the reverse order, in which Q_{A1} is executed first, incurs no penalty (as shown in Fig. 4.4d).

Example 4.1 calls for an alternative scheduling approach which takes deadlines into consideration. In this work, AFIT leverages the different available slacks to extend that basic cost-benefit comparison and inject EDF-like deadline-aware scheduling into the query selector decision. In particular, the AFIT query selector employs the following criterion for query execution: *Q_{S1} is executed first if it meets the following condition:*

$$w_{A1}\alpha_{A1}[max(0, QC_{S1} - max(0, ts_{A1}^a))] < w_{S1}[\alpha_{S1}max(0, QC_{A1} + UC_{A1} - max(0, ts_{S1}^s)) + (1 - \alpha_{S1})max(0, QC_{A1} + UC_{A1} - max(0, ss_{S1}))]$$
(4.10)

Otherwise, Q_{A1} is the one scheduled for execution.

Equation 4.10 compares the estimated penalty achieved by two different sequences: (1) $Q_{S1} \rightarrow Q_{A1}$ (i.e., Q_{S1} followed by Q_{A1}), and (2) $Q_{A1} \rightarrow Q_{S1}$ (i.e., Q_{A1} followed by Q_{S1}). Accordingly, it selects for execution the query that yields the lower penalty to the system (if any). Those two alternative execution orders are illustrated in Figs. 4.5 and 4.6 and are further discussed next.

- $Q_{S1} \rightarrow Q_{A1}$: We estimate the tardiness experienced by Q_{A1} due to waiting for Q_{S1}'s execution according to the cases shown in Fig. 4.5 and listed below:

  - $ts_{A1}^a < 0$: Fig. 4.5a shows the case in which Q_{A1} has already missed its tardiness deadline TD_{A1} regardless the execution order. Hence, waiting for Q_{S1} to finish execution increases Q_{A1}'s tardiness by QC_{S1}.

- $0 < ts_{A1}^a < QC_{S1}$: Fig. 4.5b shows that Q_{A1} has enough slack that it will incur no tardiness if it was to be executed before Q_{S1}. However, waiting for Q_{S1} to finish execution increases Q_{A1}'s tardiness by $QC_{S1} - ts_{A1}^a$.
- $0 < QC_{S1} < ts_{A1}^a$: Fig. 4.5c shows that Q_{A1} has large enough slack that it will incur no tardiness regardless of its execution order. Hence, waiting for Q_{S1} to finish execution leads to no increase in Q_{A1}'s tardiness.

Hence, the increase in total penalty $P_{S \to A}$ due to Q_{S1}'s execution is computed as: $w_{A1}\alpha_{A1}max(0, QC_{S1} - max(0, ts_{A1}^a))$, which is the left-hand component of Eq. 4.10.

- $Q_{A1} \to Q_{S1}$: Similar to the first sequence, the increase in QoS penalty experienced by Q_{S1} due to Q_{A1}'s execution is $w_{S1}\alpha_{S1}max(0, QC_{A1} + UC_{A1} - max(0, ts_{S1}^s))$. In addition, the increase in Q_{S1}'s staleness is discussed in following three cases:

  - $ss_{S1} < 0$: Fig. 4.6a shows the case in which Q_{S1} has already missed its staleness deadline SD_{S1} regardless of the execution order. Hence, waiting for Q_{A1} to finish execution increases Q_{S1}'s staleness by $QC_{A1} + UC_{A1}$.
  - $0 < ss_{S1} < QC_{A1} + UC_{A1}$: Fig. 4.6b shows that Q_{S1} will incur no stalness if it was to be executed before Q_{A1}. However, waiting for Q_{A1} to finish execution increases Q_{S1}'s staleness by $QC_{A1} + UC_{A1} - ss_{S1}$.
  - $0 < QC_{A1} + UC_{A1} < ss_{S1}$: Fig. 4.6c shows that Q_{S1} will incur no staleness regardless of its execution order. Hence, waiting for Q_{A1} to finish execution leads to no increase in Q_{S1}'s staleness.

Hence, the increase in total penalty $P_{A \to S}$ due to Q_{A1}'s execution is the right-hand component of Eq. 4.10.

Algorithm 4.4: Framework of AFIT

---

1 **while** *true* **do**
2   **foreach** *new arrival query* $Q_{i,k}$ **do**
3 | QueryRouter($Q_{i,k}$); // the condition in Section. 4.4.1
4   **end**
5   Adjust();
6     $Q_{A1} \leftarrow$ head of AL, $Q_{S1} \leftarrow$ head of SL;
7     $Q_e \leftarrow$ QuerySelector(Q_{A1}, Q_{S1}); // the condition in Section. 4.4.2
8   execute Q_e;
9 **end**

Based on the discussion, if $P_{S \to A} < P_{A \to S}$, i.e., satisfies Eq. 4.10, Q_{S1} is executed first.

Fig. 4.5 Q_{A1}'s tardiness incurred by Q_{S1}. **a** $ts_{A1}^a < 0$. **b** $0 < ts_{A1}^a < QC_{S1}$. **c** $0 < QC_{S1} < ts_{A1}^a$

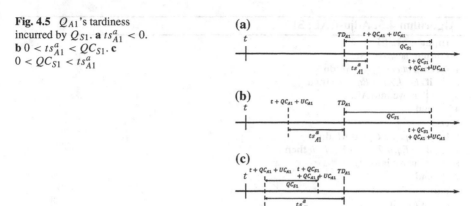

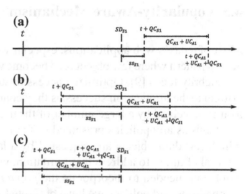

Fig. 4.6 Q_{S1}'s Staleness Incurred by Q_{A1}. **a** $ss_{S1} < 0$. **b** $0 < ss_{S1} < QC_{A1} + UC_{A1}$. **c** $0 < QC_{A1} + UC_{A1} < ss_{S1}$

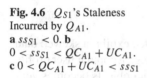

4.4.3 WSJF-AFIT

Putting it together, Algorithm 4.4 outlines the general framework of AFIT. In particular, the AFIT query router places each newly arriving query into either AL or SL (line 3). Further, at each scheduling point, AFIT would maintain both AL and SL where some queries might be shuffled between the two lists by calling the *Adjust()* procedure (line 5). Finally, the AFIT query selector will compare the two queries with the highest priority in and SL and the winner is scheduled for execution (line 7). In our implementation, AL and SL are maintained as two heaps.

Algorithm 4.5: Adjust(AL, SL)

Input : AL, SL
Output: new AL, SL
1 **foreach** *query* $Q_{i,k} \in SL$ **do**
2 | **if** *Eq. 4.7a* $\vee$ *Eq. 4.7b* **then**
3 | | move into AL;
4 | **end**
5 **end**
6 **foreach** *query* $Q_{i,k} \in AL$ **do**
7 | **if** $\neg$ *Eq. 4.7a* $\wedge$ $\neg$ *Eq. 4.7b* **then**
8 | | move into SL;
9 | **end**
10 **end**
11 **return** AL, SL ;

4.5 Popularity-Aware Mechanism

Most of today's web applications, especially social networks, exhibit a skewed data access pattern where few objects can become very popular (e.g., a popular user profile or celebrity feed) [9]. Optimized access to such popular data objects becomes very critical to the application success as they contribute significantly to the performance as it is perceived by a large number of the user population. However, the scheduling mechanisms and policies presented so far are all oblivious to that skewed pattern in which few data objects are requested by a large number of queries during a short interval of time. To address this limitation, in this section, we present the necessary extensions needed to incorporate the *popularity* of a data object in the scheduling mechanisms and policies we have presented so far.

Algorithm 4.6 shows the general framework for the popularity-aware mechanisms. In particular, in these mechanisms, the scheduler groups together the queries that are currently pending in the system queue into several groups according to the requested data objects (line 2). For instance, if queries $Q_{2,k}$, $Q_{5,k}$, and $Q_{10,k}$ are all the currently pending queries for data object O_k, then these queries are grouped together as $\mathbb{Q}_k$. Then a single priority value is assigned to each group of queries $\mathbb{Q}_k$ (or equivalently, to each data object O_k) (line 3–5). The updates on the object accessed by the group with the highest priority are installed according to the high-level mechanism, i.e., OD, HOD, or FIT (line 8). Finally, the group of queries with the highest priority is selected for execution (line 9). Next, we describe the details for computing that popularity-aware priority value for the policies presented in the previous sections.

Algorithm 4.6: Framework for *Popularity-aware* Mechanism

---

1 **while** *true* **do**
2   group the queries in current query queue by data object to be $\{\mathbb{Q}_1, \mathbb{Q}_2, \cdots, \mathbb{Q}_n\}$;
3   **foreach** *group* $\mathbb{Q}_k$ *in* $\{\mathbb{Q}_1, \mathbb{Q}_2, \cdots, \mathbb{Q}_n\}$ **do**
4 | $V_k \leftarrow$ the priority of queries on data object O_k;
5   **end**
6     $\mathbb{Q}_y \leftarrow$ the query group with the highest priority;
7     $O_y \leftarrow$ the data object accessed by $\mathbb{Q}_y$;
8   process the update on O_y;   `// according to the update model and`
         `mechanism`
9   execute the queries in group $\mathbb{Q}_y$ and remove them from the query queue;
10 **end**

4.5.1 Populairty-Aware WSJF-OD

Under the popularity-aware version of WSJF-OD, the priority of all the queries in the query group $\mathbb{Q}_k$ is computed as

$$V_k = \frac{\sum_{Q_{i,k} \in \mathbb{Q}_k} \alpha_i w_i}{QC_k} \tag{4.11}$$

where $\mathbb{Q}_k$ is the current set of pending queries on object O_k, as explained above. Hence, under the new popularity-aware WSJF-OD, the benefit of answering a group of queries $\mathbb{Q}_k$ is simply the sum of the weights of all the queries in $\mathbb{Q}_k$ (i.e., $\sum_{Q_{i,k} \in \mathbb{Q}_k} \alpha_i w_i$); whereas, the cost incurred in answering $\mathbb{Q}_k$ is basically the cost of accessing O_k once (i.e., QC_k).

4.5.2 Populairty-Aware WSJF-HOD

Similarly, to incorporate popularity under the WSJF policy of the hybrid on-demand mechanism (i.e., WSJF-HOD), the priority of all the queries in a query group $\mathbb{Q}_k$ is simply computed as

$$V_k = \frac{\sum_{Q_{i,k} \in \mathbb{Q}_k} \alpha_i w_i}{QC_k + UC_k} \tag{4.12}$$

where UC_k is the processing cost to apply the latest update on data object O_k as described in Sect. 3.1.4. Thus, the cost incurred in answering $\mathbb{Q}_k$ includes not only the cost of accessing O_k (i.e., QC_k), but also the cost of installing the latest update on O_k (i.e., UC_k).

4.5.3 Popularity-Aware WSJF-FIT

The popularity-aware version of WSJF-FIT follows the same logic presented in FIT mechanism. However, the popularity of a data objects has to be incorporated at both the local and global decisions of the scheduler. In particular, at the local-level, in order to decide whether an update to a particular data object should be skipped or installed, we compute the two penalties $\hat{P}_S$ and $\hat{P}_I$ as follows:

$$\hat{P}_S = \sum_{Q_{i,k} \in \mathbb{Q}_k} [(\tau + QC_k - TD_i)^+ \alpha_i w_i + (\tau + QC_k - SD_i)^+ (1 - \alpha_i) w_i] \quad (4.13)$$

$$\hat{P}_I = \sum_{Q_{i,k} \in \mathbb{Q}_k} (\tau + QC_k + UC_k - TD_i)^+ \alpha_i w_i \quad (4.14)$$

Notice that the group of queries in $\mathbb{Q}_k$ are expected to have different deadlines and weights for both tardiness and staleness. Additionally, those requirements are often in conflict across the different queries in $\mathbb{Q}_k$. For instance, some of the queries to the same data object O_k might have tight deadlines while others might have more relaxed deadlines. Accordingly, each of the equations above integrates all these often conflicting requirements into the an overall penalty value, where most of the contribution comes from the subset of queries in $\mathbb{Q}_k$ with tight deadlines, high weights, or both.

At the global-level, the priority V_k of a query group $\mathbb{Q}_k$ has also two possible values, namely $(V_k)^I$ and $(V_k)^S$, as follows:

$$(V_k)^I = \frac{\sum_{Q_{i,k} \in \mathbb{Q}_k} \alpha_i w_i}{QC_k + UC_k}, \qquad (V_k)^S = \sum_{Q_{i,k} \in \mathbb{Q}_k} (V_{i,k})^S \quad (4.15)$$

In particular, $(V_k)^I$ is simply computed as the counterpart of the popularity-aware WSJF-HOD; whereas, the value $(V_k)^S$ of a query group $\mathbb{Q}_k$ is simply equal to the sum of all the $(V_{i,k})^S$ values of each query $Q_{i,k} \in \mathbb{Q}_k$.

4.5.4 Popularity-Aware WSJF-AFIT

As illustrated above, popularity-aware mechanism considers query groups rather than individual queries. Meanwhile, different from the other mechanism, AFIT deliveries queries into two lists. Hence, in order to adopt AFIT conveniently, popularity-aware WSJF-FIT employs a virtual [10] query $Q_{i,k}$ which captures the properties in query group $\mathbb{Q}_k$. This virtual query includes the main parameters as follows:

- Query weight w_x: the maximum query weight among all the query in group $\mathbb{Q}_k$, i.e., $w_x = max_{Q_{i,k} \in \mathbb{Q}_k} w_i$.

- QoS preference α_x: the maximum QoS preference among all the query in group $\mathbb{Q}_k$, i.e., $\alpha_x = max_{Q_{i,k} \in \mathbb{Q}_k} \alpha_i$.
- Tardiness deadline TD_x: the minimum tardiness deadline among all the query in group $\mathbb{Q}_k$, i.e., $TD_x = min_{Q_{i,k} \in \mathbb{Q}_k} TD_i$.
- Staleness deadline SD_x: the minimum staleness deadline among all the query in group $\mathbb{Q}_k$, i.e., $SD_x = min_{Q_{i,k} \in \mathbb{Q}_k} SD_i$.

Hence, this virtual query could be used to schedule according to AFIT mechanism in Sect. 4.4.

4.6 Experimental Study

While there are many variants of key-value stores (e.g., PNUTS [11], Dynamo [12], Cassandra [13], and BigTable [14]), none of them includes all the design aspects that we have considered in this work. Moreover, while some of those data stores are open source, other are proprietary (e.g., PNUTS which implements the timeline consistency model employed in this work). Hence, we have implemented a simulation platform, which focuses primarily on the design aspects influencing the latency and freshness provided at the data store nodes. In the following, Sect. 4.6.1 describes the baseline policies in our simulation platform, Sect. 4.6.2 illustrates the parameter settings in simulation platform, and the experimental results are presented in Sect. 4.6.3–4.6.6.

The arrival of queries is modeled as a poisson process, such that the perceived load is determined by tuning the arrival rate of the poisson distribution.

4.6.1 Baseline Policies

In addition to the WSJF policy, our simulated platform also includes three baseline policies: FCFS, EDF, and Density. Table 4.1 summarizes all the combinations of mechanisms and policies presented in our experiments. Here, since FCFS and EDF are oblivious to the processing costs of both queries and updates, they can only be employed under OD mechanisms. In the following, we provide more details on those baseline policies.

The FCFS Policy: First-come-first-served (FCFS) has been proposed as the scheduling policy of choice under the OD mechanism in [4]. Under this policy, each query $Q_{i,k}$ is assigned a priority $V_{i,k} = \frac{1}{A_i}$, where A_i is the arrival time of query $Q_{i,k}$. In order to incorporate popularity, the default FCFS priority functions is extended into: $V_k = \frac{1}{min_{Q_{i,k} \in \mathbb{Q}_k} \{A_i\}}$, where $min_{Q_{i,k} \in \mathbb{Q}_k} \{A_i\}$ is the minimum (i.e., earliest) arrival time among all the queries that belong to the query group $\mathbb{Q}_k$.

Table 4.1 Mechanisms and policies

Policies	Mechanisms			
	OD	HOD	FIT	AFIT
FCFS	FCFS-OD			
EDF	EDF-OD			
Density	Density-OD	Density-HOD	Density-FIT	Density-AFIT
WSJF	WSJF-OD	WSJF-HOD	WSJF-FIT	WSJF-AFIT

The EDF Policy: Earliest deadline first (EDF) is one clear alternative for replacing FCFS under the OD mechanism. Under EDF-OD, each query $Q_{i,k}$ is assigned a priority $V_{i,k} = \frac{1}{TD_i}$, where TD_i is the tardiness deadline of query $Q_{i,k}$. To incorporate popularity, similar to FCFS, we extend the default EDF priority function to consider the minimum deadline among each group of queries. Hence, the popularity-aware version of EDF employs the following priority function: $V_k = \frac{1}{min_{Q_{i,k} \in \mathbb{Q}_k}\{TD_i\}}$, where $min_{Q_{i,k} \in \mathbb{Q}_k}\{TD_i\}$ is the minimum (i.e., earliest) tardiness deadline among all the queries that belong to the query group $\mathbb{Q}_k$.

The Density Policy: The density policy is very similar to WSJF except that it considers the momentary value of the penalty function rather than its long-term slope [7]. In particular, at each scheduling point, the density policy makes its decision based on the penalty values incurred at the current point of time. Hence, in the density priority function, the weight w_i is scaled by $(\tau + QC_k - TD_i)^+$ where τ is the current system time when a scheduling decision is to be made and in turn, $\tau + QC_k$ is the time when query $Q_{i,k}$ is expected to finish execution. Hence, when employing the density policy under the OD mechanism, the priority of query $Q_{i,k}$ is simply computed as $V_{i,k} = \frac{-\alpha_i w_i \times (\tau + QC_k - TD_i)^+}{QC_k}$. Notice that if $\tau + QC_k \leq TD_i$, then $Q_{i,k}$ is expected to finish before its deadline and the current incurred penalty is 0. However, if $\tau + QC_k > TD_i$, then $Q_{i,k}$ is expected to miss its deadline and the current incurred penalty is the weighted tardiness $w_i \alpha_i \times (\tau + QC_k - TD_i)$ or equivalently, the system benefit is the negative of that value as reflected in the priority function. Further, to incorporate popularity, that default priority function is extended to: $V_k = \frac{-\sum_{Q_{i,k} \in \mathbb{Q}_k} \alpha_i w_i (\tau + QC_k - TD_i)^+}{QC_k}$. The priority functions for Density-HOD and Density-FIT are derived similar to WSJF-HOD and WSJF-FIT, respectively.

4.6.2 Parameter Setting

The simulated data store hosts 1000 data objects with id ranging from 1 to 1000. The query generator generates 5000 queries are generated where the data object accessed by each query is determined according to a *Zipf* distribution over the range [1, 1000]. In the default setting, the skewness θ_q of this *Zipf* distribution is zero (i.e., uniform distribution over the stored data objects). To specify the QoS and QoD requirement, each query is assigned a weight w_i uniformly distributed over the range [1, 10] which represents the importance of that query. The QoS fraction of the weight (i.e., α_i) is set according to a *Zipf* distribution over the range [0, 1.0] with a default skewness of zero (i.e., uniform). The query processing cost QC_k for each query $Q_{i,k}$ depends on the accessed data object and is generated according to a uniform distribution over the range [10, 20] ms. Each query $Q_{i,k}$ is assigned a tardiness tolerance $\gamma_i^t = \sigma_i \times QC_k$, where σ_i is generated uniformly over the range [1, σ_{max}]. Hence, the tardiness deadline $TD_i = A_i + \sigma_i * QC_k$, where we set $\sigma_{max} = 10$ in our experiments. Setting the tardiness tolerance γ_i^t to be a function of the processing cost QC_k allows for generating realistic deadlines [7], which are proportional to the processing requirements. Each query $Q_{i,k}$ is also assigned a staleness tolerance γ_i^s, which is generated uniformly in range [0, 100] ms. Hence, the staleness deadline of $Q_{i,k}$ is $SD_i = R_k + \gamma_i^s$ where R_k is the timestamp of the first unapplied update to data object O_k. Table 4.2 summarizes the parameters as well as settings which are independent on update models. In other words, those parameters and settings are suited for both state-transfer and operation-transfer updates. However, the updates under these two models are different from each other, so that the parameters as well as settings depended on updates are not the same.

In our experiments on the state-transfer update model, the processing cost UC_k of each update $U_{j,k}$ is generated according to a *Zipf* distribution over the range [5, 25] ms. The skewness of *Zipf* allows us to control the impact of updates on the system load. In the default setting, *Zipf* parameter for skewness θ_u is 0.3 and skewed toward the high end of the cost range so that to reflect that the cost of a write is typically higher than that of a read. The arrival of updates is modelled as a poisson process, where we set the arrival rate to 20 updates/sec. Table 4.3 lists the special parameters and settings for state-transfer updates.

Table 4.2 Parameters and default settings independent on updates

Parameter	Value
Number of data objects	1000
Number of queries	5000
Query distribution	*Zipf* over [1, 1000], $\theta_q = 0$
Data object access cost (QC_k)	Uniform over [10, 20] ms
Tardiness parameter (σ_{max})	10
Staleness tolerance (γ_i^s)	Uniform over [0, 100] ms
Importance weight (w_i)	Uniform over [1, 10]
QoS fraction (α_i)	*Zipf* over [0, 1.0], $\theta_\alpha = 0$

Table 4.3 Parameters and default settings under state-transfer updates

Parameter	Value
Query arrival rate	5–50 queries/sec
Update arrival rate	20 updates/sec
Update cost (UC_k)	*Zipf* over [5, 25] ms,
	$\theta_u = 0.3$

4.6.3 Impact of Query Arrival Rate

In this experiment, we study the sensitivity of the different schedulers to the increase in query arrival rate. In particular, we increase the query arrival rate from 5 queries/second to 50 queries/second. Clearly, this increase in arrival rate is equivalent to an increase in perceived load (i.e., utilization). Figure 4.7 shows the incurred penalty of all the schedulers listed in Table 4.1 under state-transfer model. Figure 4.7a, b show that in general, for all schedulers the penalty increases with increasing the query arrival rate (i.e., increasing utilization). However, FCFS (i.e., the policy employed by the original OD mechanism) exhibits the highest penalty. Meanwhile, the performance of EDF comes as expected where the penalty increases significantly at high utilization because of the well-known *domino effect* [10]. That is, queries keep missing their deadlines in a cascaded fashion. The cause of this effect is that EDF might give high priority to a query with an early deadline which it has already missed, instead of scheduling another query which has a later deadline that could still be met [15].

Figure 4.7 also shows that WSJF-OD outperforms density-OD. For example, at 50 queries/sec, WSJF-OD reduces the penalty by 31 % compared to density-OD. The reason is that WSJF-OD considers the slope of the penalty function, whereas density-OD considers the instantaneous value of the penalty function as described in Sect. 4.6.1. Thus, density-OD might favor a query that seems to currently incur high penalty over another query which will incur much higher penalty in the future in case it is not scheduled for execution. It is noticeable that Fig. 4.7 shows density-AFIT

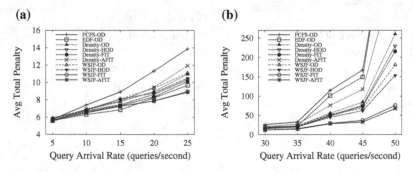

Fig. 4.7 Impact of query arrival rate: average penalty. **a** Low query rate. **b** High query rate

Fig. 4.8 Impact of query
arrival rate: normalized
penalty

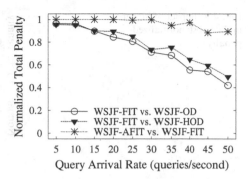

performs bad, since AFIT is tailored based on the trade-off between EDF and SJF
rather than density policy.

In Fig. 4.8, we focus our attention on comparing the performance of the different
mechanisms discussed in this work. In particular, we use the same settings for the
results shown in Fig. 4.7, but we include only the WSJF policy. First, Fig. 4.8 shows
that HOD mechanism performs better than OD mechanism, since HOD considers
the properties of both query and update. For instance, at query arrival rate of 40
queries/sec, WSJF-FIT reduces the incurred penalty by 45 % compared to WSJF-
OD. Then, Fig. 4.8 shows that FIT mechanism outperforms HOD mechanism, since
FIT might selectively decide to skip some updates if the benefit of an update does
not justify its cost, so as to save resources that might be needed by other queries
and updates. For instance, at query arrival rate of 40 queries/sec, WSJF-FIT reduces
the incurred penalty by 35 % compared to WSJF-HOD. In addition, the result above
clearly shows that the FIT mechanism performs better than OD mechanism. Finally,
Fig. 4.8 shows AFIT mechanism outperforms FIT mechanism, since AFIT accounts
for the deadline into scheduling. For instance, at query arrival rate of 50 queries/sec,
WSJF-AFIT reduces the incurred penalty by 10 % compared to WSJF-FIT.

4.6.4 Impact of Update Cost

In order to understand the interplay between queries and updates, in this experiment
we kept the same default settings as in the previous one except for increasing the
skewness of the update cost *Zipf* distribution from 0.3 to 1.7. This leads to more
updates being expensive and requiring more resource to refresh the stale data.

The results for that setting are illustrated in Fig. 4.9, in which the general performance patterns are similar to that in Fig. 4.8. However, Fig. 4.9 shows larger reductions in penalty achieved by FIT, compared to the OD and HOD mechanism. For
instance, at query arrival rate of 40 queries/sec, the reduction in penalty provided by
WSJF-FIT versus WSJF-OD is 53 % (in comparison to only 45 % in Fig. 4.8). That
increase in reduction is mainly because WSJF-FIT recognizes those queries with

Fig. 4.9 Impact of higher
update cost: normalized
penalty

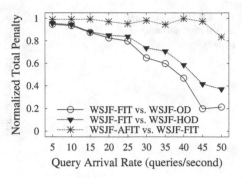

Query Arrival Rate (queries/second)

expensive update processing cost and will either skip the updates so that to give high
priority or, like WSJF-HOD, assign queries low priority in order to favor the other
queries and updates with lower costs. In addition, Fig. 4.9 shows AFIT performs better than FIT under this settings. For instance, at query arrival rate of 50 queries/sec,
WSJF-AFIT reduces the incurred penalty by 17 % compared to WSJF-FIT.

4.6.5 Impact of Different QoS and QoD Preferences

To further illustrate the trade-off between QoS (i.e., tardiness) and QoD (i.e., staleness), in this experiment we keep the same default values except for changing the
skewness parameter, i.e., θ_α, of the QoS preference *Zipf* distribution. In particular,
we increase θ_α from 0.0 to 1.7 which is skewed toward high values of α_i. This leads
to more queries giving a higher preference to QoS over QoD, which in turn results
in more penalty for violating tardiness deadlines than staleness deadlines.

Figure 4.10 shows our experimental results under that setting in which the benefits
achieved by the FIT mechanism are further emphasized. For instance, in Fig. 4.10
at query arrival rate of 40 queries/sec, WSJF-FIT reduces the penalty by 58 % compared to WSFJ-OD and by 51 % compared to WSFJ-HOD (vs. only 45 and 35 %
under the settings for Fig. 4.8). This increase in gain (or equivalently reductions in
penalty) is due to WSJF-FIT dynamically skipping updates that correspond to queries
assigning low weight to QoD, i.e., more interested in QoS as expressed by their α_i
settings. In addition, Fig. 4.10 shows AFIT performs better than FIT under this settings. For instance, at query arrival rate of 50 queries/sec, WSJF-AFIT reduces the
incurred penalty by 14 % compared to WSJF-FIT. Generally, the penalty reduction
by WSJF-AFIT versus WSJF-FIT in Fig. 4.10 is more than the one in Fig. 4.8. WSJF-
AFIT could not only dynamically skip updates like WSJF-FIT, but also account for
deadline, so that to schedule queries with a high QoS preference.

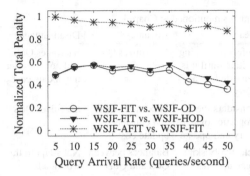

Fig. 4.10 Impact of higher QoS preference: normalized penalty

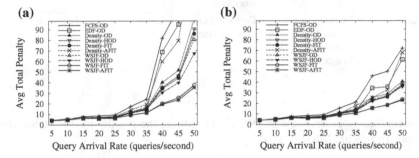

Fig. 4.11 Impact of popularity: average penalty. **a** Popularity-neutral (default). **b** Popularity-aware

4.6.6 Impact of Popularity

As described before, the queries in simulation platform are generated according to a *Zipf* distribution with θ_q as the skewness parameter. In the default setting, the skewness θ_q is zero (i.e., uniform distribution over the stored data objects); whereas in this experiment, we set $\theta_q = 0.8$ which brings forth a skewed query workload under which some data objects are more popular than others.

Figure 4.11a shows the results provided by all the default schedulers, which are popularity-neutral (i.e., oblivious to popularity); whereas Fig. 4.11b shows the result of popularity-aware schedulers. In general, popularity-aware schedulers exhibit much lower penalty compared to the default ones. For example, lets consider the case of query rate 40 queries/sec. In that case, the popularity-aware FCFS-OD (Fig. 4.11b) reduces the total penalty by 44 % in comparison to the default FCFS-OD (Fig. 4.11a). Similarly, the popularity-aware WSJF-FIT (Fig. 4.11b) reduces the total penalty by 20 % in comparison to the default WSJF-FIT (Fig. 4.11a). This shows that leveraging popularity improves the performance of all the schedulers. Moreover, Fig. 4.11b shows that FIT and AFIT continues to outperform OD and HOD when popularity is taken into consideration. For instance, the figure shows that at query arrival rate of

Table 4.4 The mechanisms mentioned in Chap. 4

Mechanism	Idea	Advantage	Disadvantage	Section
OD	Defers refreshing an itme until it is requested by a query	Maximizes QoD	Sacrifices QoS and not consider the update cost	Section 4.1
HOD	Considers the properties of query and update	Maximizes QoD and considers update cost	Sacrifices QoS	Section 4.2
FIT	Selectively skips some updates	Balances between QoS and QoD	Not adapt to the workloads	Section 4.3
AFIT	Considers deadline by slacks	Dynamically adapts to the workloads	Not consider data popularity	Section 4.4
Popularity	Groups queries according to requested data objects	Considers the data popularity		Section 4.5

40 queries/sec, popularity-aware WSJF-FIT reduces the penalty by 30 % compared to popularity-aware WSJF-OD.

4.7 Summary

In this chapter, we study the quality-aware scheduling for state-transfer updates. The first five sections illustrate on-demand (OD) mechanism (Sect. 4.1), hybrid on-demand (HOD) mechanism (Sect. 4.2), freshness/tardiness (FIT) mechanism (Sect. 4.3), adaptive freshness/tardiness (AFIT) mechanism (Sect. 4.4), and popularity-aware mechanism (Sect. 4.5). Table 4.4 summarizes the main idea and advantage as well as disadvantage of those mechanisms. In addition, we describe the designing of simulation platform and provide experimental analysis based on this platform to explore the scheduling strategies for state-transfer updates (Sect. 4.6).

References

1. Xu, C., Sharaf, M.A., Zhou, M., Zhou, A., Zhou, X.: Adaptive query scheduling in key-value data stores. DASFAA **1**, 86–100 (2013)
2. Xu, C., Sharaf, M.A., Zhou, X., Zhou, A.: Quality-aware schedulers for weak consistency key-value data stores. Distrib. Parallel Databases **32**(4), 535–581 (2014)
3. Per Hansen, B. (ed.): Classic Operating Systems: From Batch Processing to Distributed Systems. Springer, New York (2000)

4. Adelberg, B., Garcia-Molina, H., Kao, B.: Applying update streams in a soft real-time database system. In: SIGMOD Conference, pp. 245–256 (1995)
5. Thomas, R.H.: A majority consensus approach to concurrency control for multiple copy databases. ACM Trans. Database Syst. **4**(2), 180–209 (1979)
6. Buttazzo, G.C., Spuri, M., Sensini, F.: Value vs. deadline scheduling in overload conditions. In: RTSS, pp. 90–99 (1995)
7. Haritsa, J.R., Carey, M.J., Livny, M.: Value-based scheduling in real-time database systems. VLDB J. **2**(2), 117–152 (1993)
8. Zhu, Y., Sharaf, M.A., Zhou, X.: Scheduling with freshness and performance guarantees for web applications in the cloud. In: ADC, pp. 133–142 (2011)
9. Silberstein, A., Terrace, J., Cooper, B.F., Ramakrishnan, R.: Feeding frenzy: selectively materializing users' event feeds. In: SIGMOD Conference, pp. 831–842 (2010)
10. Guirguis, S., Sharaf, M.A., Chrysanthis, P.K., Labrinidis, A., Pruhs, K.: Adaptive scheduling of web transactions. In: ICDE, pp. 357–368 (2009)
11. Cooper, B.F., Ramakrishnan, R., Srivastava, U., Silberstein, A., Bohannon, P., Jacobsen, H.-A., Puz, N., Weaver, D., Yerneni, R.: Pnuts: Yahoo!'s hosted data serving platform. PVLDB **1**(2), 1277–1288 (2008)
12. DeCandia, G., Hastorun, D., Jampani, M., Kakulapati, G., Lakshman, A., Pilchin, A., Sivasubramanian, S., Vosshall, P., Vogels, W.: Dynamo: Amazon's highly available key-value store. In: SOSP, pp. 205–220 (2007)
13. Lakshman, A., Malik, P.: Cassandra: a decentralized structured storage system. Oper. Syst. Rev. **44**(2), 35–40 (2010)
14. Chang, F., Dean, J., Ghemawat, S., Hsieh, W.C., Wallach, D.A., Burrows, M., Chandra, T., Fikes, A., Gruber, R.E.: Bigtable: a distributed storage system for structured data. ACM Trans. Comput. Syst. **26**(2) (2008)
15. Sharaf, M.A., Chrysanthis, P.K., Labrinidis, A., Amza, C.: Optimizing i/o-intensive transactions in highly interactive applications. In: SIGMOD Conference, pp. 785–798 (2009)

Chapter 5
Scheduling for Operation-Transfer Updates

Abstract Under the operation-transfer update model, the propagated updates involve partial content rather than the entire value. Hence, each replica basically reconstructs the current value of a data object from a history of propagated updates. This manner is suited for key-value stores such as PNUTS, Cassandra, and BigTable with a schema-like structured values where the value component is divided into columns as in traditional row structures and the system is responsible for the semantic interpretation of the read and write operations. Under operation-transfer updates, each data object in key-value stores accessed by its key still leads to a clear relationship between the arriving queries and their corresponding pending updates. In this chapter (Part of this chapter are reprinted from Xu et al., Distrib Parallel Databases 32(4): 535–581, 2014 [1], with kind permission from Springer Science+Business Media.), based on an operation-transfer model for update propagation, we present scheduling strategies for the efficient processing of both pending queries and updates at key-value data store nodes. In the following, Sect. 5.1 describes hybrid on-demand (HOD) mechanism; Sect. 5.2 presents freshness/tardiness (FIT) mechanism; Sect. 5.3 introduces popularity-aware mechanism; Sect. 5.4 shows the experimental analysis based on a simulation platform; Sect. 5.5 summarizes this chapter.

Keywords Operation-transfer · Scheduling Mechanism · Scheduling Policy · Experiment

5.1 Hybrid On-Demand (HOD) Mechanism

Under the operation-transfer model, the master node propagates a sequence of operations to each replica. In turn, each replica applies the received operations to its local state [2]. Hence, each replica basically reconstructs the current value of a data object from a history of propagated updates. Operation-transfer can be more efficient than state-transfer when the data objects are large and operations happen at a high level, such as writes to certain columns in the value component of structured data stores. For instance, Cassandra employs *RowMutation* to apply a set of update operations on a certain row [3]. Those operations are basically the modifications needed to bring the value component of the row to complete freshness.

© The Author(s) 2015   65
C. Xu and A. Zhou, *Quality-aware Scheduling for Key-value Data Stores*,
SpringerBriefs in Computer Science, DOI 10.1007/978-3-662-47306-1_5

Algorithm 5.1: RefreshOperationTransfer(O_k)//Complete Refreshing

---
Input : data object O_k
Output: new data object O_k
1 $\mathbb{U} = \{U_{1,k}, U_{2,k}, \ldots, U_{n,k}\}$ ← updates on the data object O_k ;
2 **foreach** $U_{j,k} \in \mathbb{U}_k$ **do**
3 | $O_k \leftarrow Q_k + U_{j,k}$;// refresh data object O_k
4 **end**
5 **return** O_k ;

As in Algorithm 5.1, bringing a data object to freshness under the operation-transfer model requires installing all its pending updates as opposed to only installing the latest one under the state-transfer mode. In this section, we also refer to the total update cost of object O_k as UC_k. However, under the operation-transfer model studied in this section, the update cost UC_k is variable and is defined as

$$UC_k = \Theta_k + l_k * \Delta_k \qquad (5.1)$$

Equation 5.1 is a typical representation of variable cost model in which l_k represents the number of operations (i.e., pending updates) on data object O_k; whereas, Θ_k and Δ_k reflect the static and dynamic components of that cost model. In particular, Δ_k represents the CPU and in-memory costs for processing each of those l_k pending updates; whereas, Θ_k represents the I/O cost which is incurred only once when those updates are applied together in a batch.

The OD mechanism as well as WSJF-OD strategy under operation-transfer updates is the same as the one under state-transfer updates, since the scheduling decision in OD is purely query-based and the computation of priority is clearly independent of the update propagation model. Hence, in this section, we extend the HOD mechanism for the operation-transfer model. The idea of this mechanism is to defer refreshing an object until it is requested by a query and consider the characteristics of updates in addition to those of queries during scheduling decision. On the one hand, Algorithm 4.1 is directly applicable to the operation-transfer model. In particular, refreshing the data object O_k should install all the updates on O_k by calling Algorithm 5.1. On the other hand, the policy along with HOD mechanism would consider update cost when computing priority according to Eq. 5.1. In this following, we introduce weighted shortest job first (WSJF) policy combined with HOD mechanism, i.e., WSJF-HOD strategy, under operation-transfer updates.

5.1.1 WSJF-HOD

Since HOD mechanism defers refreshing an object until it is requested by a query, installing updates has QoS impact rather than QoD impact on following queries. In particular, processing a certain update with cost UC_k leads to delaying the processing of each query in the system by an amount of time equals to UC_k, which might lead to an increase in the overall tardiness. However, it has no impact on the QoD since data objects are always refreshed before they are read.

For the HOD mechanism, the extension is fairly simple and straightforward. In particular, it needs to consider the new update cost for the operation-transfer model described above. For instance, in the operation-transfer version of WSJF-HOD, a query $Q_{i,k}$ on data object O_k is assigned a priority as follows:

$$V_{i,k} = \frac{\alpha_i w_i}{QC_k + (\Theta_k + l_k * \Delta_k)} \tag{5.2}$$

where Θ_k, l_k and Δ_k are as described earlier.

5.2 Freshness/Tardiness (FIT) Mechanism

In this section, we extend the FIT mechanism for the operation-transfer model. As described in previous chapter, FIT is based on the basic idea of the selective applying of updates. In the operation-transfer model discussed in this section, the selectivity in applying updates becomes further complicated due to the variability in the number of pending updates to each data object. In particular, the decision goes beyond the simple binary decision of installing or skipping the latest update to the more general case of deciding the optimal number m of updates to install per object before it is accessed. Hence, two clear special cases would be to skip all updates (i.e., $m = 0$) or to install all updates (i.e., $m = l_k$). In the general case, however, given a query $Q_{i,k}$, the FIT scheduler needs to make two main decisions as shown in Algorithm 5.2:

1. *Local decision:* what is the number of pending updates m that are to be applied to data object O_k? (line 3); and
2. *Global decision:* how to assign an appropriate priority to each query so that to minimize the overall system penalty? (line 4)

To address the first requirement above, we need to choose a value m ($0 \leq m \leq l_k$), which minimizes the penalty perceived by a query $Q_{i,k}$ that accesses data object O_k. This task is more involved than its counterpart in the state-transfer model because of the many possible choices of m. In particular, increasing m leads to increasing the update cost while at the same time decreasing the staleness of O_k.

Clearly, the impact of m on the update cost is linear and straightforward to compute. To measure the impact of m on staleness, we first need to extend our definition of staleness deadline $SD_{i,k}$ to accommodate the case of multiple pending updates. Specifically, given a data object O_k with a sequence of unapplied pending updates $\mathbb{U}_k = U_k^0, U_k^1, \ldots, U_k^{l_k-1}$, we define R_k^x as the timestamp of the xth update to object O_k. That is, R_k^x is the arrival time of the update U_k^x. Hence, given a query $Q_{i,k}$ to object O_k with a staleness tolerance γ_i^s, the staleness deadline for $Q_{i,k}$ depends on

---

Algorithm 5.2: Framework for FIT in Operation-Transfer Update Model

---

1 **while** *true* **do**
2 │ **foreach** *query $Q_{i,k}$ in current query queue* **do**
3 │ │ $m \leftarrow$ the number of update operations on O_k to install;
4 │ │ $(V_{i,k})^m \leftarrow$ the priority of $Q_{i,k}$ based on m;
5 │ **end**
6 │ $Q_{x,y} \leftarrow$ the query with the highest priority;
7 │ $m \leftarrow$ the number of update operations on O_y to install;
8 │ **if** $m > 0$ **then**
9 │ │ `RefreshOperationTransfer` (O_y, m); `// call Algorithm 5.3`
10 │ **end**
11 │ execute $Q_{x,y}$ and remove it from the query queue;
12 **end**

Algorithm 5.3: RefreshOperationTransfer(O_k, m)//Partial Refreshing

---

Input : data object O_k
Output: new data object O_k
1 $U = \{U_{1,k}, U_{2,k}, \ldots, U_{n,k}\} \leftarrow$ updates on the data object O_k ;
2 **while** $m > 0$ **do**
3 │ $O_k \leftarrow Q_k + U_{j,k}$; `// refresh data object` O_k
4 │ $m \leftarrow m - 1$;
5 **end**
6 **return** O_k ;

---

the number of updates that are installed before executing $Q_{i,k}$. Consequently, we define the *dynamic staleness deadline* $SD_{i,k}^m$ as:

$$SD_{i,k}^m = \begin{cases} R_k^m + \gamma_i^s & \text{if } m = 0, 1, \ldots, l_k - 1 \\ \infty & \text{if } m = l_k \end{cases} \tag{5.3}$$

where m is the number of updates installed before executing $Q_{i,k}$ (i.e., updates $U_k^0, U_k^1, \ldots, U_k^{m-1}$), and R_k^m is the arrival time of the mth update (i.e., first unapplied update).

For instance, Fig. 5.1 shows a sequence of pending updates with arrival times $R_k^0, R_k^1, \ldots, R_k^{l_k-1}$. In Fig. 5.1a, no update is installed (i.e., $m = 0$), hence the timestamp of the first unapplied update is R_k^0 and the dynamic staleness deadline is set accordingly as $SD_{i,k}^0 = R_k^0 + \gamma_i^s$. Meanwhile, Fig. 5.1b shows an example in which a subsequence of m updates have been installed, hence the first unapplied update is R_k^m and the dynamic staleness deadline has advanced to $SD_{i,k}^m = R_k^m + \gamma_i^s$. Finally, in Fig. 5.1c, all the updates are installed ($m = l_k$) and the dynamic staleness deadline becomes infinite (i.e., $Q_{i,k}$ receives 100 % freshness regardless of when it is executed unless new updates arrive).

Given the above definition of dynamic staleness deadline (Eq. 5.3), the total penalty incurred for $Q_{i,k}$ is computed as follows:

Fig. 5.1 Dynamic staleness deadline. Reprinted from Ref. [1], with kind permission from Springer Science+Business Media. **a** $m = 0$. **b** $0 < m < l_k$. **c** $m = l_k$

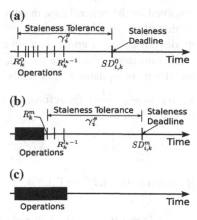

$$
\hat{P}_m =
\begin{cases}
(\tau + QC_k - TD_i)^+ \alpha_i w_i + (\tau + QC_k - SD^0_{i,k})^+(1 - \alpha_i)w_i, \text{ if } m = 0 \\[2ex]
[\tau + QC_k + (\Theta_k + m * \Delta_k) - TD_i]^+ \alpha_i w_i \\
+ [\tau + QC_k + (\Theta_k + m * \Delta_k) - SD^m_{i,k}]^+(1 - \alpha_i)w_i, \qquad \text{if } 0 < m < l_k \\[2ex]
[\tau + QC_k + (\Theta_k + l_k * \Delta_k) - TD_i]^+ \alpha_i w_i \qquad\qquad \text{if } m = l_k
\end{cases}
\tag{5.4}
$$

Hence, for each query under the FIT mechanism, we need to find the *optimal* value of m, such that $m = \varphi$ and satisfies the following two constraints:

1. $\hat{P}_\varphi \le \hat{P}_j$, where $0 \le j \le l_k$ and
2. $\hat{P}_j > \hat{P}_\varphi$, where $\varphi < j \le l_k$.

The first constraint ensures $\hat{P}_\varphi$ is the minimum value among $\hat{P}_0, \hat{P}_1, \ldots, \hat{P}_{l_k}$. That is, we want to set m to the optimal value φ, which results in the lowest possible penalty.

The second constraint ensures that φ is assigned the largest value of all the possible values of m that minimize the penalty function $\hat{P}_m$. In particular, this constraint acts as a tiebreaker in case there are multiple values of m that can give the same optimal $\hat{P}_m$ and it breaks the ties in favor of the highest m. The intuition is that installing more updates (i.e., choosing the highest m) results in the same minimum penalty, while at the same time it increases the chances that the freshness requirements of the following queries to the updated object will be met instantly.

In order to satisfy the first constraint, we can compute $\hat{P}_0, \hat{P}_1, \ldots, \hat{P}_{l_k}$ by substitution in Eq. 5.4 to find the optimal φ. However, the computational complexity of this *exhaustive* method is $O(l_k)$, which is clearly impractical. Instead, we propose an *approximate* approach for computing φ, which is of constant complexity $O(1)$.

To this end, notice that the first and last cases of Eq. 5.4 represent the two special cases in which $m = 0$ and $m = l_k$, respectively. Clearly, it is easy to compute the estimated penalty $\hat{P}_m$ for each of those two cases, whereas the computation is more involved for the general case in which $0 < m < l_k$ because $SD_{i,k}^m$ is dependent on our choice of m. To address this problem and in order to simplify the calculations, we model the arrival of updates on a data objects O_k according to a uniform distribution with some interarrival time μ_k. The value of μ_k can then be deduced by monitoring the stream of updates and is easily estimated using a sequence of pending updates as: $\mu_k = \frac{R_k^{l_k-1} - R_k^0}{l_k - 1}$. Therefore, for $0 < m < l_k$, $SD_{i,k}^m$ can be expressed as a linear function in m as follows:

$$SD_{i,k}^m \approx R_k^0 + \mu_k * m + \gamma_i^s \tag{5.5}$$

By substituting $SD_{i,k}^m$ in Eq. 5.4, $\hat{P}_m$ at $0 < m_k < l_k$ is expressed as:

$$\hat{P}_m = \left[\tau + QC_k + (\Theta_k + m * \Delta_k) - TD_i\right]^+ \alpha_i w_i + [\tau + QC_k + (\Theta_k + m * \Delta_k) \\ -(R_k^0 + \mu_k * m + \gamma_i^s)]^+ (1 - \alpha_i) w_i \tag{5.6}$$

Now that the incurred penalty is defined in terms of the selected number of updates to be applied (i.e., m), in the following we describe our method to find the optimal value of m in constant time (i.e., $O(1)$).

Toward this, note that Eq. 5.6 can be simply represented in terms of two linear functions defined over m. In particular, we represent Eq. 5.6 as:

$$\hat{P}_m = [g_{i,t}(m)]^+ \alpha_i w_i + [g_{i,s}(m)]^+ (1 - \alpha_i) w_i = G_{i,t}(m) + G_{i,s}(m)$$

where $G_{i,t}(m)$ is the tardiness component of the penalty $\hat{P}_m$ such that $[g_{i,t}(m)]^+ = [\tau + QC_k + (\Theta_k + m * \Delta_k) - TD_i]^+$. Similarly, $G_{i,s}(m)$ is the staleness component of the penalty $\hat{P}_m$ such that $[g_{i,s}(m)]^+ = [\tau + QC_k + (\Theta_k + m * \Delta_k) - (R_k^0 + \mu_k * m + \gamma_i^s)]^+$.

Both $G_{i,t}(m)$ and $G_{i,s}(m)$ are linear functions that are defined over m and they are both monotonic. $G_{i,t}(m)$, however, is always monotonically increasing whereas $G_{i,s}(m)$ is either monotonically increasing or monotonically decreasing.

As shown in Fig. 5.2a, the value of $G_{i,t}(m)$ remains 0 as we increase m up to a certain point after which it increases linearly with m. We denote such point as the *tardiness critical point* $\Gamma_{i,t}$. Intuitively, the tardiness penalty is 0 as long as the number of installed updates (i.e., m) would not lead to missing the deadline TD_i, otherwise the tardiness penalty increases linearly with m as shown in Fig. 5.2a. Since m is a discrete value bounded in the range $[1, l_k - 1]$, $\Gamma_{i,t}$ is simply calculated as $\max(1, \min(\frac{TD_i - (\tau + QC_k + \Theta_k)}{\Delta_k}, l_k - 1))$.

The monotonicity of $G_{i,s}(m)$ on the other hand depends on the value $\Delta_k - \mu_k$. In particular, $G_{i,s}(m)$ is monotonically increasing if $\Delta_k - \mu_k > 0$ and it is monotonically decreasing otherwise. Figure 5.2b shows the monotonically increasing version of $G_{i,s}(m)$. Note that the behavior of $G_{i,s}(m)$ in this case is similar to that of $G_{i,t}(m)$ (Fig. 5.2a). In particular, Fig. 5.2b shows that the value of $G_{i,s}(m)$ remains 0 as we increase m up to a certain point after which it increases linearly with m. We

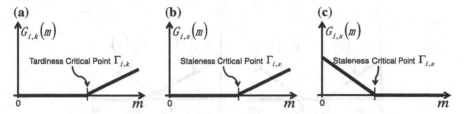

Fig. 5.2 Tardiness and staleness critical points. Reprinted from Ref. [1], with kind permission from Springer Science+Business Media. **a** $\Gamma_{i,t}$. **b** $\Gamma_{i,s}$, $\Delta_k > \mu_k$. **c** $\Gamma_{i,s}$, $\Delta_k < \mu_k$

denote such point as the *staleness critical point* $\Gamma_{i,s}$. Intuitively, in this case where $\Delta_k - \mu_k > 0$, the rate of installing the pending updates is slower than their arrival rate. Hence, installing more updates beyond $\Gamma_{i,s}$ will only lead to further missing the staleness deadline and accumulating more penalty as shown in Fig. 5.2b.

To the contrary, Fig. 5.2c shows the monotonically decreasing version of $G_{i,s}(m)$. In particular, Fig. 5.2c shows that the value of $G_{i,s}(m)$ decreases as we increase m up to the staleness critical point $\Gamma_{i,s}$ where it reaches 0 and stays there with increasing m. In this case where $\Delta_k - \mu_k > 0$, the cost of installing an update (i.e., Δ_k) is less than the updates interarrival time (i.e., μ_k), hence by installing more updates the system will eventually push the staleness deadline $SD_{i,k}$ to a point where the data staleness meets the query requirements and hence incur no staleness penalty.

In both of the cases above (Fig. 5.2b, c), similarly to computing $\Gamma_{i,t}$, m is a discrete value bounded in the range $[1, l_k - 1]$, hence $\Gamma_{i,s}$ is computed as: $\max(1,$ $\min(\frac{R_k^0 + \gamma_i^s - (\tau + QC_k + \Theta_k)}{\Delta_k - \mu_k}, l_k - 1))$.

Given the above definitions of $\Gamma_{i,t}$ and $\Gamma_{i,s}$, the optimal φ' for $\dot{P}_m$ in Eq. 5.6 is computed in constant time (i.e., $O(1)$) according to the following cases:

- If $\Delta_k \geq \mu_k$: In this case, the cost of installing an update is higher than the updates interarrival time. Hence, both $G_{i,t}(m)$ and $G_{i,s}(m)$ monotonically increase after the tardiness critical point $\Gamma_{i,t}$ and the staleness critical point $\Gamma_{i,s}$, respectively. In turn, the overall penalty $\hat{P}_m$ will start to monotonically increase at the point where m is equal to the minimum of $\Gamma_{i,t}$ and $\Gamma_{i,s}$. Therefore, $\varphi' = \min(\Gamma_{i,t}, \Gamma_{i,s})$.

- If $\Delta_k < \mu_k$: In this case, the cost of installing an update is less than the updates interarrival time. Hence, $G_{i,s}(m)$ monotonically decreases before the staleness critical point $\Gamma_{i,s}$ whereas $G_{i,t}(m)$ monotonically increases after tardiness critical point $\Gamma_{i,t}$. Clearly, this case can be further depicted into two sub-cases according to the relationship between $\Gamma_{i,s}$ and $\Gamma_{i,t}$, which is shown in Fig. 5.3a, b and is discussed next.

  - If $\Gamma_{i,s} \leq \Gamma_{i,t}$: This case is illustrated in Fig. 5.3a, in which the combined overall penalty $\hat{P}_m$ decreases when $m \leq \Gamma_{i,s}$ and increases when $m \geq \Gamma_{i,t}$. In between $\Gamma_{i,s}$ and $\Gamma_{i,t}$, $\hat{P}_m$ is equal to 0. Therefore, $\varphi' = \Gamma_{i,t}$.

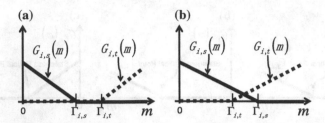

Fig. 5.3 The relationship between the tardiness and staleness critical points. Reprinted from Ref. [1], with kind permission from Springer Science+Business Media. **a** $\Gamma_{i,s} \leq \Gamma_{i,t}$. **b** $\Gamma_{i,s} > \Gamma_{i,t}$

– **If $\Gamma_{i,s} > \Gamma_{i,t}$:** This case is illustrated in Fig. 5.3b, in which the combined overall penalty $\hat{P}_m$ behaves similarly to the previous case as it decreases when $m \leq \Gamma_{i,t}$ and increases when $m \geq \Gamma_{i,s}$. However, in between $\Gamma_{i,t}$ and $\Gamma_{i,s}$, $\hat{P}_m$ is a linear function and its monotonicity depends on the relationship between the slopes of $G_{i,t}(m)$ and $G_{i,s}(m)$. Let's denote that linear function in the range $[\Gamma_{i,t}, \Gamma_{i,s}]$ as $\hat{p}_m$. Accordingly, $\hat{p}_m = [g_{i,t}(m)]\alpha_i w_i + [g_{i,s}(m)](1 - \alpha_i)w_i$ and its first derivative is equal to $w_i(\Delta_k - \mu_k(1 - \alpha_i))$. Hence,

If $\Delta_k > \mu_k(1 - \alpha_i)$, then $\hat{p}_m$ is monotonically increasing, and accordingly $\varphi' = \Gamma_{i,t}$.

If $\Delta_k \leq \mu_k(1 - \alpha_i)$, then $\hat{p}_m$ is monotonically decreasing, and accordingly $\varphi' = \Gamma_{i,s}$.

From the discussion above, for each pending query $Q_{i,k}$, we can now calculate the value φ' in $O(1)$. Finally, the obtained $\hat{P}_{\varphi'}$ is compared with the two special cases $\hat{P}_0$ and $\hat{P}_{l_k}$ to get the final φ per query, i.e., the optimal number of updates to be installed before the query is executed.

5.2.1 WSJF-FIT

At this point, the high-level FIT mechanism provides an efficient solution for making the local decision listed earlier in this section. That is, finding the number of pending updates m that are to be applied to each requested data object O_k. The solution to the global decision (i.e., assigning an appropriate priority to each query) is handled by the low-level scheduling policy similar to the state-transfer FIT. Next, we describe the extensions needed to our previously proposed WSJF-FIT policy in order to accommodate the operation-transfer model.

In the special case in which the FIT mechanism decides that for a certain query $Q_{i,k}$ the optimal number of updates to install is $m = 0$, then all the pending updates corresponding to that query are to be skipped. Hence, the priority of that query is computed based on Fig. 4.1 and is denoted as $(V_{i,k})^0$ (as $(V_{i,k})^S$ in Sect. 4.3.1). In the general case in which $m > 0$, then the cost for applying those m updates is modeled as: $\Theta_k + m * \Delta_k$ (as previously defined in Eq. 5.1). Hence, the final priority of each query $Q_{i,k}$ is computed as follows:

$$(V_{i,k})^m = \frac{\alpha_i w_i}{QC_k + (\Theta_k + m * \Delta_k)}, m = 1, 2, \ldots, l_k$$

$$(V_{i,k})^0 = \begin{cases} \frac{w_{im}}{QC_{kq}} & \tau \leq D_{il} \\ \frac{w_i}{QC_{kq}} & \tau > D_{il} \end{cases}$$

In particular, $(V_{i,k})^m$ at $m = l_k$ is the same as Eq. 5.2. Hence, $(V_{i,k})^m$ describes a more general case.

5.3 Popularity-Aware Mechanism

In this section, we present our popularity-aware scheduling mechanisms and policies for the operation-transfer model. Algorithm 4.6 is also applicable to depict popularity-aware mechanism under operation-transfer updates. It follows the following simple steps:

1. find query group $\mathbb{Q}_k$ on object O_k which has the highest priority (line 2–6),
2. apply all the pending updates to O_k (line 8), and
3. serve O_k to all the pending queries in $\mathbb{Q}_k$ that have requested it (line 9).

The popularity-aware mechanism groups the different queries that access the same object O_k in a group $\mathbb{Q}_k$ and the scheduling decision is made based on the overall requirements of all the queries in $\mathbb{Q}_k$. However, the scheduling decision should also account for the presence of multiple pending updates to the accessed data objects as it is typical under the operation-transfer mode and as explained in the previous sections. To this end, in the following we revisit the strategies we have proposed under the operation-transfer model and extend them into their popularity-aware version, namely: popularity-aware WSJF-HOD and WSJF-FIT.

5.3.1 Popularity-Aware WSJF-HOD

As it has been the convention throughout this work, the priority of each object is computed according to the low-level scheduling policy. In the case where the WSJF policy is employed under the hybrid on-demand mechanism (i.e., WSJF-HOD), the priority of the queries in group $\mathbb{Q}_k$ on data object O_k is computed as:

$$V_k = \frac{\sum_{Q_{i,k} \in \mathbb{Q}_k} \alpha_i w_i}{QC_k + (\Theta_k + l_k * \Delta_k)} \tag{5.7}$$

where the sum of all the query weights reflects the benefit obtained from answering all the queries in $\mathbb{Q}_k$ and the cost incurred consists of two components: the cost to install all the pending updates to O_k (i.e., $\Theta_k + l_k * \Delta_k$) and the cost to access data object O_k after it has been updated (i.e., QC_k).

5.3.2 Popularity-Aware WSJF-FIT

Under the FIT mechanism, in addition to selectively deciding the optimal number of updates to be installed to each object O_k, a popularity-aware version will also have to account for the disparate requirements of the different queries requesting O_k (i.e., $\mathbb{Q}_k$). Hence, the total perceived penalty per object O_k is computed as follows:

$$\hat{P}_m = \begin{cases} \sum_{Q_{i,k} \in \mathbb{Q}_k} [(\tau + QC_k - TD_i)^+ \alpha_i w_i + \\ (\tau + QC_k - SD_{i,k}^0)^+ (1 - \alpha_i) w_i] & \text{if } m = 0 \\ \\ \sum_{Q_{i,k} \in \mathbb{Q}_k} ([\tau + QC_k + (\Theta_k + m * \Delta_k) - TD_i]^+ \alpha_i w_i \\ + [\tau + QC_k + (\Theta_k + m * \Delta_k) - SD_{i,k}^m]^+ (1 - \alpha_i) w_i) & \text{if } 0 < m < l_k \\ \\ \sum_{Q_{i,k} \in \mathbb{Q}_k} [\tau + QC_{kq} + (\Theta_k + l_k * \Delta_k) - TD_i]^+ \alpha_i w_i & \text{if } m = l_k. \end{cases} \tag{5.8}$$

Clearly in the equation above, the penalty is evaluated based on all the tardiness and staleness deadline of the queries in $\mathbb{Q}_k$ so that to incorporate popularity. However, this makes finding an exact solution (i.e., finding optimal φ for m) a complex task. In an exhaustive approach, we can compute $\hat{P}_0, \hat{P}_1, \ldots, \hat{P}_{l_k}$ by substitution in Eq. 5.8 to find the optimal φ at a high computational complexity of $O(|\mathbb{Q}_k| \times l_k)$ where $|\mathbb{Q}_k|$ is the number of queries in group $\mathbb{Q}_k$. To reduce this complexity to $O(|\mathbb{Q}_k|)$, in the following we employ approximations similar to the ones applied to Eq. 5.4 in addition to further approximations to deal with the impact of considering a group of queries $\mathbb{Q}_k$ instead of individual queries.

Firstly, by applying the previous approximation of $SD_{i,k}^m$ described in Eq. 5.5, $\hat{P}_m$ for the case where $0 < m < l_k$ is simplified to:

$$\hat{P}_m = \sum_{Q_{i,k} \in \mathbb{Q}_k} [\tau + QC_k + (\Theta_k + m * \Delta_k) - TD_i]^+ \alpha_i w_i$$
$$+ \sum_{Q_{i,k} \in \mathbb{Q}_k} [\tau + QC_k + (\Theta_k + m * \Delta_k) - (R_k^0 + \mu_k * m + \gamma_i^s)]^+ (1 - \alpha_i) w_i$$

$$(5.9)$$

By employing $[g_{i,t}(m)]^+$ and $[g_{i,s}(m)]^+$ defined in the previous section,

$$\hat{P}_m = \sum_{Q_{i,k} \in \mathbb{Q}_k} [g_{i,t}(m)]^+ \alpha_i w_i + \sum_{Q_{i,k} \in \mathbb{Q}_k} [g_{i,s}(m)]^+ (1 - \alpha_i) w_i$$

Here, $\sum_{Q_{i,k} \in \mathbb{Q}_k} [g_{i,t}(m)]^+ \alpha_i w_i$ is the aggregated tardiness component of the penalty $\hat{P}_m$ and we denote it as $\mathbb{G}_t(m)$. Similarly, $\sum_{Q_{i,k} \in \mathbb{Q}_k} [g_{i,s}(m)]^+ (1 - \alpha_i) w_i$ is the aggregated staleness component of $\hat{P}_m$, which we denote as $\mathbb{G}_s(m)$. Hence, $\hat{P}_m = \mathbb{G}_t(m) + \mathbb{G}_s(m)$.

As shown in Fig. 5.4, the monotonicity behavior of $\mathbb{G}_t(m)$ and $\mathbb{G}_s(m)$ is similar to that of $G_{i,t}(m)$ and $G_{i,s}(m)$, respectively. Additionally, as it has been the case for $G_{i,t}(m)$ and $G_{i,s}(m)$, this monotonicity is defined in terms of two critical points: Γ_t and Γ_s, respectively. However, notice that both $\mathbb{G}_t(m)$ and $\mathbb{G}_s(m)$ are *piecewise linear* functions defined over m as opposed to the purely linear ones shown in Fig. 5.2.

In particular, $\mathbb{G}_t(m) = \sum_{Q_{i,k} \in \mathbb{Q}_k} G_{i,t}(m)$ and $\mathbb{G}_s(m) = \sum_{Q_{i,k} \in \mathbb{Q}_k} G_{i,s}(m)$, where $G_{i,t}(m)$ and $G_{i,s}(m)$ are as defined in Sect. 5.2. Hence, as shown in Fig. 5.4a, Γ_t of $\mathbb{G}_t(m)$ is $\min_{Q_{i,k} \in \mathbb{Q}_k}(\Gamma_{i,t})$, i.e., the minimum tardiness critical point for the queries in $\mathbb{Q}_k$. Similarly, if $\Delta_k > \mu_k$, then Γ_s of $\mathbb{G}_s(m)$ is $\min_{Q_{i,k} \in \mathbb{Q}_k}(\Gamma_{i,s})$, i.e., the minimum staleness critical point for the queries in $\mathbb{Q}_k$ (as shown in Fig. 5.4b), whereas if $\Delta_k < \mu_k$, then Γ_s of $\mathbb{G}_s(m)$ is $\max_{Q_{i,k} \in \mathbb{Q}_k}(\Gamma_{i,s})$.

Given those two critical points, the optimal value of m (i.e., φ') for Eq. 5.9 is computed as follows:

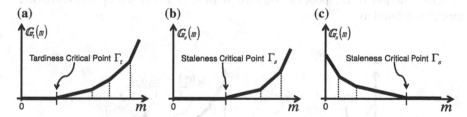

Fig. 5.4 Tardiness and staleness critical points for a group of queries. Reprinted from Ref. [1], with kind permission from Springer Science+Business Media. **a** Γ_t. **b** Γ_s, $\Delta_k > \mu_k$. **c** Γ_s, $\Delta_k < \mu_k$

- **If** $\Delta_k \geq \mu_k$: This case is shown in Fig. 5.4a, b in which both $\mathbb{G}_s(m)$ and $\mathbb{G}_t(m)$ are monotonically increasing after the tardiness critical point Γ_t and the staleness critical point Γ_s, respectively. In turn, $\hat{P}_m$ will start to monotonically increase at the point where m is equal to the minimum of Γ_t and Γ_s. Therefore, $\varphi' = min(\Gamma_t, \Gamma_s)$.
- **If** $\Delta_k < \mu_k$: In this case $\mathbb{G}_s(m)$ is illustrated as in Fig. 5.4c, whereas $\mathbb{G}_t(m)$ resembles Fig. 5.4a. This case is further depicted into two sub-cases according to the relationship between Γ_t and Γ_s, which are shown in Fig. 5.5a, b, respectively.

  - **If** $\Gamma_s \leq \Gamma_t$: as illustrated in Fig. 5.5a, the overall penalty $\hat{P}_m$ decreases when $m \leq \Gamma_s^k$ and increases when $m \geq \Gamma_t^k$. Between Γ_s and Γ_t, $\hat{P}_m$ equals to 0. Therefore, $\varphi' = \Gamma_t$.
  - **If** $\Gamma_s > \Gamma_t$: as illustrated in Fig. 5.5b, similar to previous case, the overall penalty $\hat{P}_m$ decreases when $m \leq \Gamma_t$ and increases when $m \geq \Gamma_s$. However, the monotonicity of $\hat{P}_m$ in the range $[\Gamma_t, \Gamma_s]$ cannot be easily determined due to the piecewise linearity. Thus, for simplicity, we use linear functions to approximate that piecewise linearity (as shown in Fig. 5.5b). That is, $\frac{\mathbb{G}_t(\Gamma_s)}{\Gamma_s - \Gamma_t}$ estimates the slope for $\mathbb{G}_t(m)$, whereas $\frac{\mathbb{G}_s(\Gamma_t)}{\Gamma_s - \Gamma_t}$ estimates the slope for $\mathbb{G}_s(m)$. Accordingly,

    If $\frac{\mathbb{G}_t(\Gamma_s)}{\Gamma_s - \Gamma_t} > \frac{\mathbb{G}_s(\Gamma_t)}{\Gamma_s - \Gamma_t}$, $\hat{P}_m$ is estimated to monotonically increase with m. Therefore, $\varphi' = \Gamma_t$.

    If $\frac{\mathbb{G}_t(\Gamma_s)}{\Gamma_s - \Gamma_t} \leq \frac{\mathbb{G}_s(\Gamma_t)}{\Gamma_s - \Gamma_t}$, $\hat{P}_m$ is estimated to monotonically decrease with m. Therefore, $\varphi' = \Gamma_s$.

The obtained $\hat{P}_{\varphi'}$ is compared with the two special cases $\hat{P}_0$ and $\hat{P}_{l_k}$ to get the optimal φ, i.e., the optimal number of updates to be installed. The popularity-aware FIT mechanism presented above can be summarized using Algorithm 4.6. In particular, at line 8, $m = \varphi$ update operations are installed in the operation-transfer model for FIT.

Finally, we present the popularity-aware WSJF low-level scheduling policy that works in synergy with the FIT mechanism for the operation-transfer model. The priority function of the popularity-aware WSJF-FIT under the operation-transfer model is defined as

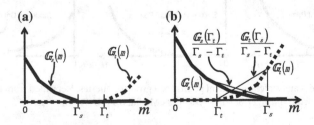

Fig. 5.5 Relationship between staleness and tardiness critical points for a group of queries. Reprinted from Ref. [1], with kind permission from Springer Science+Business Media. **a** $\Gamma_s \leq \Gamma_t$. **b** $\Gamma_s > \Gamma_t$

$$(V_k)^m = \begin{cases} \dfrac{\sum_{Q_{i,k} \in \mathbb{Q}_k} \alpha_i w_i}{QC_k + (\Theta_k + m * \Delta_k)} & m = 1, 2, \ldots, l_k \\ \\ \sum_{Q_{i,k} \in \mathbb{Q}_k} (V_{i,k})^0 & m = 0 \end{cases}$$

Intuitively, if all of the updates are to be skipped (i.e., $m = 0$) then the priority of a data object O_k is equal to the sum of $(V_{i,k})^0$, where the priority of each individual query is computed as in the WSJF-FIT policy presented in the previous section. In the general case in which $m > 0$, the priority of each data object resembles that of the popularity-aware WSJF-HOD except that it considers the impact of applying only m updates as opposed to all updates (i.e., l_k).

5.4 Experimental Study

In this section, we present the results for the operation-transfer updates based on our simulated experimental platform. Differently from the state-transfer updates, bringing a data object to freshness under the operation-transfer updates requires installing all its pending updates as opposed to only installing the latest one. Hence, the arrival rate of updates plays an important role in shaping the exhibited performance. Accordingly, in the next set of experiments, we primarily evaluate the sensitivity of the different schedulers to the variability in update arrival rate rather than query arrival rate as in the previous chapter.

5.4.1 Parameter Setting

The parameters as well as their settings in Table 4.2 are independent on update propagation. Those parameters could be adopted in experiments for both state-transfer and operation-transfer updates. Hence, in this section, we also employ those parameters in experiment for operation-transfer updates. In our experiments on the operation-transfer model, the update cost of a data object O_k is calculated according to $UC_k = \Theta_k + l_k * \Delta_k$. That is, the total update cost of O_k is the sum of I/O cost (i.e., Θ_k) and CPU cost (i.e., Δ_k). In our default setting, Θ_k is uniformly generated over the range [5, 15] ms and Δ_k is uniformly distributed in range [1, 3] ms so that to maintain the ratio between the I/O and CPU costs in the reasonable range of [5, 15]. In order to further study the impact of operation-transfer updates, the arrival of updates is modeled as a poisson process and we vary the expected arrival rate from 20 to 200 updates/s. The number of pending updates per data object O_k is expected to increase as we increase update rate. Table 5.1 lists the settings of parameters for operation-transfer updates.

Table 5.1 Parameter setting
for operation-transfer updates

Parameter	Value
Query arrival rate	25 queries/s
Update arrival rate	20–200 updates/s
IO cost (Θ_k)	Uniform over [5, 15] ms
CPU cost (Δ_k)	Uniform over [1, 3] ms

5.4.2 Impact of Update Arrival Rate

In this experiment, we vary the update arrival rate from 20 to 200 updates/s, whereas
the query arrival rate is set to 25 queries/s. All other parameters are set to their default
values. Figure 5.6 shows the performance provided by the different schedulers.

Figure 5.6 shows that for all schedulers, the incurred penalty increases with
increasing the update arrival rate. As expected, this is similar to the pattern exhibited
previously when increasing the query arrival rate (Fig. 4.7). Among all the schedulers
shown in Fig. 5.6, WSJF-FIT provides the lowest penalty. In Fig. 5.7, we further study
the performance of the SJF-based schedulers. In general, Fig. 5.7 shows that WSJF-
FIT provides lower penalty than both WSJF-HOD and WSJF-OD. For instance, at
update arrival rate of 100 updates/s, WSJF-FIT provides penalty reduction around
23 % compared to WSJF-HOD and 31 % compared to WSJF-OD. Note that all the
FIT schedulers plotted in this figure employ an *exhaustive* approach to determine
the optimal number of updates to apply. In the next Sect. 5.4.3, we compare that
approach to the *approximate* one for estimating the number of applied updates.

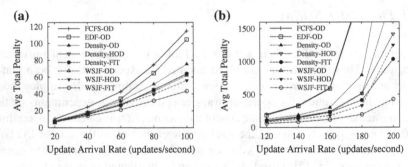

Fig. 5.6 Impact of update arrival rate: average penalty. Reprinted from Ref. [1], with kind permission from Springer Science+Business Media. **a** Low update rate. **b** High update rate

Fig. 5.7 Impact of update arrival rate: normalized penalty. Reprinted from Ref. [1], with kind permission from Springer Science+Business Media

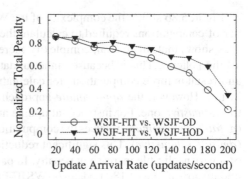

5.4.3 Impact of Popularity and Approximation

In this experiment, we employ the same setting as in Sect. 5.4.2 to evaluate the impact of approximation when estimating the number of applied updates. Moreover, we also evaluate the impact of popularity by setting $\theta_q = 0.8$ which brings forth a skewed query workload.

For clarity of presentation, the schedulers evaluated in this experiment are summarized as follows: (1) WSJF-FIT (*default, exhaustive*) (Sect. 5.2), (2) WSJF-FIT (*default, approximate*) (Sect. 5.2), (3) WSJF-FIT (*popularity, exhaustive*) (Sect. 5.3.2), and (4) WSJF-FIT (*popularity, approximate*) (Sect. 5.3.2).

In Fig. 5.8a, similar to the state-transfer model, the popularity-aware FIT under the operation-transfer exhibits much lower system penalty compared to the default ones. For instance, at update arrival rate of 180 updates/s, WSJF-FIT (*popularity, exhaustive*) reduces the total penalty by 15 % in comparison to WSJF-FIT (*default, exhaustive*). In addition, Fig. 5.8a shows that the performance of WSJF-FIT (*default, approximate*) and WSJF-FIT (*popularity, approximate*) is very close to that of WSJF-FIT (*default, exhaustive*) and WSJF-FIT (*popularity, exhaustive*), respectively.

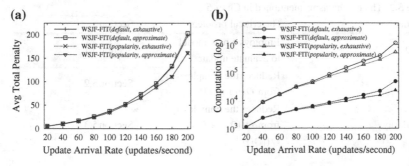

Fig. 5.8 Impact of popularity and approximation. Reprinted from Ref. [1], with kind permission from Springer Science+Business Media. **a** Avgerage penalty. **b** Number of computations

Figure 5.8b shows the complexity of the WSJF-FIT schedulers which is the number of computations required to calculate the number of installed updates. That figures shows that, in general, complexity increases along with update arrival rate for all the policies. This is because higher update arrival rates will bring more updates and result in more computations for calculating the number of update operations to install. However, the *approximate* approach clearly incurs less computations than the *exhaustive* one. For instance, at update arrival rate of 180 updates/s, WSJF-FIT (*default*, *approximate*) reduces the computations by 95 % in comparison to WSJF-FIT (*default*, *exhaustive*). This significant reduction in complexity comes at the expense of a very negligible increase in penalty. In particular, as Fig. 5.8a shows, at the same update arrival rate of 180 updates/s, WSJF-FIT (*default*, *approximate*) increases the penalty by only 1.5 % in comparison to WSJF-FIT (*default*, *exhaustive*).

5.5 Summary

In this chapter, we study the quality-aware scheduling under operation-transfer updates, including hybrid on-demand (HOD) mechanism (Sect. 5.1), freshness/tardiness (FIT) mechanism (Sect. 5.2), and popularity-aware mechanism (Sect. 5.3). The idea of these mechanisms is the same as the ones in the previous chapter. However, the key problems to tackle under operation-transfer updates has new features listed in Table 5.2. Notice that, on-demand (OD) mechanism under operation-transfer updates is the same as the one under state-transfer updates. In addition, adaptive freshness/tardiness (AFIT) mechanism would have to maintain a number of query list rather than only AL and SL, if it were applied under operation-transfer updates. Hence, we do not explore AFIT under operation-transfer updates since it is too complex. Finally, we provide experimental analysis based simulated platform to study the scheduling strategies for operation-transfer updates (Sect. 5.4).

Table 5.2 The mechanisms mentioned in Chap. 5

Mechanism	The critical problem	Section
HOD	Employs a new model to evaluate update	Section 5.1
FIT	Reduces the complexity from $O(l_k)$ to $O(1)$	Section 5.2
Popularity	Reduces the complexity from $O(|\mathbb{Q}_k| \times l_k)$ to $O(|\mathbb{Q}_k|)$	Section 5.3

References

1. Xu, C., Sharaf, M.A., Zhou, X., Zhou, A.: Quality-aware schedulers for weak consistency key-value data stores. Distrib. Parallel Databases **32**(4), 535–581 (2014)
2. Saito, Y., Shapiro, M.: Optimistic replication. ACM Comput. Surv. **37**(1), 42–81 (2005)
3. Hewitt, E.: Cassandra: The Definitive Guide. O'Reilly Media Inc., Sebastopol (2010)

Chapter 6
AQUAS: A Quality-Aware Scheduler

Abstract In order to study the role of quality-aware scheduling in practice, we introduce a quality-aware scheduler named AQUAS (Xu et al., AQUAS: a quality-aware scheduler for NoSQL data stores 1210–1213, 2014 [1]) which has been integrated into Cassandra. This prototype employs the strategies proposed in previous chapters to manage the quality-aware scheduling in key-value stores. In particular, AQUAS extends the Cassandra API to allow application developers to specify quality-aware parameters, and implements a task scheduling component as well as a cost estimation component. In addition, we propose a modified YCSB (Coopre et al., Benchmarking cloud serving systems with YCSB 143–154, 2010 [2]) to evaluate AQUAS prototype, and explore the timeline query in miroblogging application to demonstrate the role of quality-aware scheduling based on AQUAS prototype. In the following, Sect. 6.1 describes the design of a quality-aware scheduler named AQUAS; Sect. 6.2 illustrates a benchmark named QCSB, which is tailored for AQUAS, as well as the performance study; Sect. 6.3 takes the timeline query on Microblogging application as a example, to depict the application supported by AQUAS; Sect. 6.4 summaries this chapter.

Keywords Prototype · AQUAS · Evaluation · Demonstration

6.1 System Overview

In key-value data stores, data is typically organized in tables or tablets of rows where each row is an abstract key-value pair. In particular, Cassandra supports eventual consistency to manage replicas of the same key-value pair. It also provides asynchronous replication in which replica updates are propagated in a lazy manner. In other words, the write operations to some replicas are disseminated in the background. Hence, a replica object is accessed by either a foreground read request (i.e., user query) or a background write request (i.e., system update). Additionally, each Cassandra instance starts and manages a fixed number of threads to execute read or write tasks. In our proposed prototype, AQUAS continuously schedules those foreground reads and background writes at each replica, in order to maximize the user satisfaction in both QoS and QoD.

© The Author(s) 2015

C. Xu and A. Zhou, *Quality-aware Scheduling for Key-value Data Stores*,
SpringerBriefs in Computer Science, DOI 10.1007/978-3-662-47306-1_6

6.1.1 System Goals

To quantify QoS, *service-level agreement (SLA)* has been widely used to specify the
expectations and tolerance for latency. Intuitively, SLA acts as a *soft* deadline where
delays beyond the prespecified SLA incur penalties to the system. AQUAS allows
application developers to configure a QoS penalty function of the form as

$$f(A_i, \gamma_i^t, F_i, \alpha_i, w_i) \tag{6.1}$$

where A_i is the query arrival time, γ_i^t is a tardiness tolerance, F_i is the finish time,
w_i is query weight and α_i is tardiness factor (i.e., QoS preference). Here, a common
choice for f is a linear piecewise function [3] as in Definition 3.3. That is,

$$f(A_i, \gamma_i^t, F_i, \alpha_i, w_i) = \begin{cases} \alpha_i w_i [F_i - (A_i + \gamma_i^t)] & \text{if } F_i > A_i + \gamma_i^t \\ 0 & \text{otherwise} \end{cases} \tag{6.2}$$

In addition, we adopt a *Freshness Level Agreement (FLA)* for specifying QoD
in terms of freshness. Similar to SLA, FLA describes the user's expectations for
freshness in serviced data. Generally, providing stale data could reduce delays and
satisfy the prespecified SLAs requirements; whereas, updating the requested data
before serving it could improve freshness but incur additional delays. Similar to
QoS, AQUAS allows application developers to configure QoD penalty function as

$$g(R_k, \gamma_i^s, F_i, \alpha_i, w_i) \tag{6.3}$$

where R_k is the timestamp of the first unapplied update to O_k update and γ_i^s is a
staleness tolerance. Here, a common choice for f is a linear piecewise function as
in Definition 3.6. That is,

$$g(R_k, \gamma_i^s, F_i, \alpha_i, w_i) = \begin{cases} (1 - \alpha_i) w_i [F_i - (R_k + \gamma_i^s)] & \text{if } F_i > R_k + \gamma_i^s \\ 0 & \text{otherwise} \end{cases} \tag{6.4}$$

This time-based function g mapping the time factors into QoD penalty is especially
useful in a distributed environment [4].

In AQUAS, the combined penalty incurred by a query $Q_{i,k}$ is represented as

$$P_i = f(A_i, \gamma_i^t, F_i, \alpha_i, w_i) + g(R_k, \gamma_i^s, F_i, \alpha_i, w_i) \tag{6.5}$$

Hence, for N queries, our objective is to minimize the average total penalty, i.e.,

$$\frac{1}{N} \sum_{i=1}^{N} P_i \tag{6.6}$$

6.1.2 System Design

In order to achieve that goal, AQUAS extends the API of Cassandra 1.2.5, so as to allow application developers to specify quality-aware parameters including tardiness tolerance γ_i^t, staleness tolerance γ_i^s, query weight w_i and QoS preference α_i. The modified get() is as follows:

$$get(key, \gamma_i^t, \gamma_i^s, w_i, \alpha_i)$$

In addition, AQUAS rewrites the task scheduling component and injects cost estimation component, so that to implement our scheduling strategies. Figure 6.1 shows the framework of AQUAS prototype including a task scheduler and a cost estimator. In particular, the task scheduler manages the read/write queue according to the system settings; whereas, the cost estimator evaluates the execution time of some read or write tasks to support scheduling.

6.1.2.1 Scheduling

As shown in Fig. 6.1, each node in key-value stores continuously receives user queries and system updates. Hence, a replica object is accessed by either a foreground read request (i.e., user query) or a background write request (i.e., system update). Similar to set *multiprogramming level (MPL)* [5, 6] in traditional database, each Cassandra instance starts and manages a fixed number of threads to execute read or write tasks. Those tasks are placed into corresponding read and write queues until they are

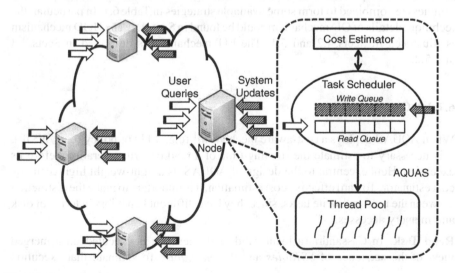

Fig. 6.1 System architecture

Table 6.1 The strategies supported in current version of AQUAS

Policy	Mechanism		
	OD	HOD	FIT
FCFS	FCFS-OD		
EDF	EDF-OD		
Density	Density-OD	Density-HOD	Density-FIT
WSJF	WSJF-OD	WSJF-HOD	WSJF-FIT

submitted to a thread pool for execution. In original Cassandra, the tasks in read or write queue are executed according to their arrival sequences (i.e., FCFS), and these two queues are independent to each other. This component is implemented by raw `ThreadPoolExecutor` in JDK.

In our prototype, AQUAS couples read and write tasks and implements a new executor of thread pool to employ the scheduling strategies proposed in this work. First, this executor adopts MaxHeap so that the read task with the highest priority locates on the top of the heap. In particular, the priority is computed according to scheduling policies. Then, AQUAS makes distinction between foreground and background writes. The foreground writes are processed according to original mechanisms; whereas, the background writes are submitted into the write queue in the new executor. This write queue is implemented by a HashMap in order to quickly search a update to access a data object. Finally, the new executor continuously picks up read tasks from read queue and searches the write task which accesses the same data object, so as to employ the mechanisms in this work.

The current version of AQUAS has implemented the mechanisms such as OD, HOD, FIT, and policies such as FCFS, EDF, and WSJF. Those mechanisms and policies are combined to form some available strategies in Table 6.1. In particular, the technique details of OD mechanism could be found in Sect. 4.1. The HOD mechanism is illustrated in Sects. 4.2 and 5.1. The FIT mechanism is described in Sects. 4.3 and 5.2.

6.1.2.2 Cost Estimation

When AQUAS deploys a cost-aware mechanism[1] (e.g., FIT) or policy (e.g., WSJF), it is necessary to estimate the running time of a read or write operation before its execution. Hence, central to the design of AQUAS, is a light-weight high-accuracy cost estimator. Toward effective cost estimation, it is important to make the distinction between the read and write tasks, since they have different behaviors in terms of disk and memory accesses.

Read Task: In Cassandra, a local valid read operation is executed on a merged view of the sequence of *SSTables* and the *memtable*. To estimate that execution

---

[1] ©[2014] IEEE. Reprinted, with permission, from Ref. [1].

time, we adopt a simple approach based on statistical estimation that leverages the monitored execution times of previous queries. In particular, this approach consists of two stages:

- *offline sampling*: AQUAS randomly samples some keys in an offline manner and records the cost (i.e., time) needed to retrieve their corresponding objects. In AQUAS, we rely on an embedded Berkley DB for the fast storage and retrieval of those costs.
- *online feedback*: During handling user queries, AQUAS captures the costs incurred in processing each of the submitted read operations. Similar to the offline stage, those costs are also recorded in Berkley DB, where older values are updated.

For cost estimation, if the cost of an input read operation exists in the database, the estimator reports that cost. Otherwise, it reports an average cost instead. Clearly, the accuracy of estimation is improved with the increase in offline sampling. However, in AQUAS, sampling is permitted when the system is idle. Meanwhile, the online feedback compensates for that drawback and refines the estimated cost.

Write Task: A local write operation in Cassandra is appended to *commit-log* on disk and delivered to *memtable* in-memory. The data in *memtable* does not leave memory until a *compaction* occurs (e.g., when *memtable* reaches a threshold). Hence, estimating the cost of a write operation is relatively simple, since in-memory operations behave linearly. This observation allows AQUAS to employ a simple linear regression model for estimating the cost of writes. The primary factors shaping that model are data size and the cost of appending onto the *commit-log*.

6.2 System Performance

YCSB (Yahoo! Cloud System benchmark) [2] is a performance evaluation tool for cloud database by Yahoo! Research. YCSB could evaluate key-value stores such as well-known HBase, Cassandra, PNUTS, Mongodb, Redis, etc. As a benchmark, YCSB reports the performances such as throughput, latency at concurrent loading, querying, or updating. In this work, we partially modify YCSB to serve as a benchmark for AQUAS. In this section, we first introduce the benchmark based on YCSB and then describe the performance results.

6.2.1 Benchmark

YCSB integrates a data generator, workload generator, workload executor, performance reporter, and database clients, etc. It provides a suite of solution to performance evaluation. In particular, the data generator generates dataset according to prespecified data distribution, record size, the number of fields, etc., whereas, the workload generator generates workloads according to prespecified ratio between different operations. YCSB is very flexible for extension, so that to be attractive since its open sourcing. It is convenient for users to define a new workload, implement a new client to evaluate a data management system, or even modify the source code to inject novel functions. On the one hand, some researchers create new database clients and extends workloads, in order to compare the performance of different data management systems in specific application scenario. For instance, employing the workloads in YCSB to simulate online advertising, electronic monitor, etc., to evaluate the performance of different key-value stores [7]. On the other hand, recent work in [8] extends the function of YCSB to conveniently observe the features of data management systems to form a comprehensive evaluation.

In order to evaluate AQUAS prototype, we propose QCSB (Quality-aware Cloud System Benchmark) which inherits from YCSB and modifies the following components:

- Workload executor: this component is responsible for workload generation such as queries, updates, and scans. Differently, QCSB generates queries along with quality-aware parameters including tardiness tolerance (γ_i^t), staleness tolerance (γ_i^s), query weight (w_i) and QoS preference (α_i). Similar to the simulation platform, these parameters are generated according to specific distributions which could be specified by command line.
- Database client: The Cassandra client in YCSB is not applicable in this context, since AQUAS extends Cassandra API. Hence, QCSB employs a new client according to AQUAS API, so as to support the evaluation for AQUAS prototype.
- Performance reporter: YCSB is able to report the performance related to query latency (i.e., the evaluation on QoS). Here, QCSB inherits this evaluation on QoS and also adds a evaluation on QoD. In particular, QCSB explores the metadata from query results to compute the data freshness, in order to report a comprehensive evaluation on both QoS and QoD.

6.2.2 Evaluation Result

For the results presented in the following,[2] we have deployed our modified Cassandra 1.2.5 on three server-class machines (dual 64-bit quad core 2.13 GHz Intel Xeon CPUs, 8 GB of RAM and gigabit ethernet). Moreover, we have generated a database and workload (i.e., queries and updates) using the Yahoo! Cloud Serving Benchmark (YCSB) [2]. The generated database consists of 600,000 records (i.e., rows) with the size of each record ranging from 1 KB to 4 MB. Further, each record is structured as a key and a set of columns with the number of columns ranging from 1 to 2000. In our setting, the replica factor is 3 and each server stores around 20 GB of data after internal compression. In term of workloads, we have experimented with YCSB workload A (update heavy) and B (read heavy) in [2]. Moreover, we have extended

---

[2]This section is reprinted from Ref. [9], with kind permission from Springer Science+Business Media.

Table 6.2 The parameters to specify QoS and QoD in QCSB

Parameter	Default setting
Tardiness tolerance (γ_i^t)	Uniform over [0, 100] (ms)
Staleness tolerance (γ_i^s)	Uniform over [0, 100] (ms)
Query weight (w_i)	Uniform over [1, 10]
QoS preference (α_i)	*Zipf* over [0, 1.0], $\theta_\alpha = 0$

the YCSB benchmark to include specifications for the QoS and QoD requirements
listed in Table 6.2, which are currently beyond the scope of YCSB. In addition, we run
the workloads mentioned above for three times and report the average performance
results next.

6.2.2.1 Penalty Versus Workloads

In this experiment, we examine the scalability of our Cassandra-based prototype system under the YCSB benchmark [2]. In order to evaluate the scalability of a data store,
YCSB introduces the notion of *offered throughput*. In particular, the YCSB workload
generator allows for specifying a targeted throughput (i.e., offered throughput), and
accordingly generates the corresponding queries and updates so that to achieve such
throughput. We note that the offered throughput parameter is an indicator of node
utilization, same as our arrival rate parameter used in the previous sections.

Figure 6.2a shows the penalty versus throughput curves for the YCSB workload A,
which has 50 % queries and 50 % updates. Similarly, Fig. 6.2b shows the performance
under the YCSB workload B, which is a query heavy workload (95 % queries and
5 % updates). The figures show that under those two typical workloads, WSJF-FIT
outperforms all the other scheduling strategies studied in this paper. For instance,
around the throughput of 1000 operations/s, WSJF-FIT reduces the incurred penalty
by 30 % compared to WSJF-OD for workload A and by 23 % for workload B.

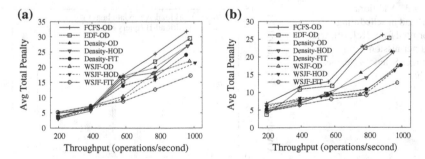

Fig. 6.2 The average penalty under two typical workloads. Reprinted from Ref. [9], with kind
permission from Springer Science+Business Media. **a** Workload A (update heavy). **b** Workload B
(query heavy)

6.2.2.2 Scheduling Overhead

It is well known that employing a scheduling strategy leads to additional overheads for computing and comparing priorities. In addition to minimizing such overheads, it is also crucial to measure their impact on the overall achieved performance so that to ensure the feasibility of scheduling. For instance, a scheduling strategy that entails high overhead is typically impractical, regardless of its desired theoretical performance.

In our prototype system implementation, we have employed several optimizations for reducing the scheduling overheads. In particular, our optimized implementation is based on the commonly used techniques of in-memory heap sort and hashing. To assess the impact of such optimizations, and the scheduling overhead in general, Fig. 6.3 shows the ratio between the incurred overheads to the total execution time (in terms of average and standard deviation). As expected, the figure shows that FCFS-OD and EDF-OD rarely incur additional overheads. The figure also shows that for the other strategies, the ratio of overhead w.r.t query execution time, is constantly below 10 % and is 5 % on average. Hence, it represents only a small fraction of the total processing requirements, which is primarily dominated by the execution of incoming operations. Such a small overhead, clearly makes for a practical implementation that allows for reaping the benefits of the proposed schedulers. For instance, under the YCSB workload A at 1000 operations/s, WSJF-FIT is able to reduce the total penalty by 47 % compared to FCFS-OD (as shown in Fig. 6.2a) at the expense of a very low overhead (as shown in Fig. 6.3).

Interestingly, Fig. 6.3 also shows that the percentage of scheduling overhead is relatively higher for workload A, which is update heavy. This is because for a cost-based scheduler, a heavy update workload leads to frequent changes in data size, which consequently incurs more overhead during the cost estimation phase (as described above). Moreover, for an update-aware scheduler (e.g., FIT), the cost of installing updates is integrated in the scheduling priority functions, which naturally requires additional computations and comparisons.

Fig. 6.3 Additional overhead in scheduling. Reprinted from Ref. [9], with kind permission from Springer Science+Business Media

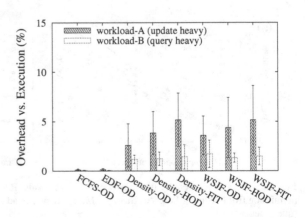

6.3 A Demonstration on MicroBlogging Application

In this section,[3] we will introduce a demonstration, i.e., a microblogging system that we have built on top of AQUAS prototype. This system will demonstrate how to support quality-aware scheduling for timeline queries on microblog. In the following, Sect. 6.3.1 describes timeline queries in AQUAS and Sect. 6.3.2 shows a case study.

6.3.1 Timeline Queries in AQUAS

Like Twitter, each user in our microblogging system has a set of followers and subscribes to a set of followees. Every time a user logs onto her account, she receives the latest microblogs (i.e., tweets) generated by her followees in the form of a list that is ordered by recency. This functionality, usually termed *timeline query*, typically involves issuing many read queries to the key-value data store so that to retrieve the latest updates generated by each followee. Clearly, a microblogging user expects a very short response time to their timeline query while also expecting to see a list that includes all the recent tweets. Moreover, microblogging applications typically host hundreds of millions of users, which makes answering simultaneous timeline queries a challenging task and requires efficient scheduling to maximize the user satisfaction in both QoS and QoD, as offered by AQUAS.

AQUAS allows application developers to set a tardiness tolerance, staleness tolerance, query weight, and QoS preference in order to specify the QoS and QoD requirements. Hence, a timeline query is expected to finish execution within the latency bound while also tolerating missing some data that fall within the staleness bound. That is, no penalty is incurred if a query finishes within the latency bound and acquires all the tweets generated beyond the staleness bound. Otherwise, there is a system penalty for violating the QoS or QoD requirement. Here, we choose piecewise linear functions to present QoS penalty function f and QoD penalty function g as shown in Eqs. 6.2 and 6.4, respectively. Our configuration interface also allows setting different quality-aware requirements to different users. For example, application developers could set tight tardiness and staleness tolerance for VIP users, whereas, general users are provided by relatively relaxed tolerances, or set a high weight for some users who are pleasure to pay fees. In such scenario, providing differentiated service is necessary and is easily achieved via our proposed AQUAS.

6.3.2 A Case Study

To illustrate the benefits of AQUAS, in our demonstration scenario we present to the audience the timeline of few representative users while running thousands of users in the background. Moreover, we employ a tweet generator that has the ability to

---

[3]©[2014] IEEE. Reprinted, with permission, from Ref. [1].

produce new tweets on the fly or to replay them from a stored log file. Figure 6.4 shows one representative user named AQUAS; whereas, Fig. 6.5 shows the portion of the tweets coming from AQUAS's followees (as produced by our generator). A tweet (including content, creation time, etc.) is stored in a super column where the tweets generated by the same user are inserted into a single row with the user id as the key. Hence, a timeline query for a certain user is implemented as reading all the tweets generated by that user followees using our modified Cassandra key-value query API.

Ideally, the tweets in Fig. 6.4 should be identical to the ones in Fig. 6.5. However, there might be some deviations based on the employed scheduler. For instance, when the scheduler skips updates (i.e., tweets) in order to minimize the total penalty incurred due to QoS/QoD requirement violation. In particular, Fig. 6.4 shows a demonstrated setting in which we set a latency bound to *5ms* and staleness bound to *1s*. Compared to Fig. 6.5, two recent tweets from user Reading are temporarily skipped by the scheduler (highlighted within bold frames). To capture the impact of such tradeoffs, we provide a monitoring tool, which allows the audience to gain

Fig. 6.4 Timeline of user AQUAS. ©[2014] IEEE. Reprinted, with permission, from Ref. [1]

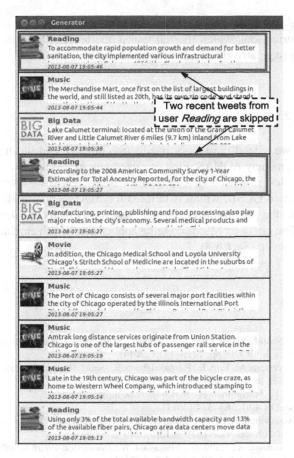

Fig. 6.5 Generating tweets from AQUAS's followees. ©[2014] IEEE. Reprinted, with permission, from Ref. [1]

Fig. 6.6 Performance metadata. ©[2014] IEEE. Reprinted, with permission, from Ref. [1]

insights into the perceived user experience. Figure 6.6 shows a sample dashboard from our monitoring tool, which lists all issued queries together with their performance metadata (e.g., arrival time, finish time, penalties, etc.).

6.4 Summary

In this chapter, we extend the theory results into practice and illustrate a quality-aware scheduler, namely AQUAS. First, we overview AQUAS prototype, including system goal and design as well as its implementation (Sect. 6.1). Then, we describe a benchmark named QCSB, which is tailored for AQUAS and modified based on YCSB, as well as the performance analysis (Sect. 6.2). Finally, we depict a demonstration of timeline query on Microblogging application, which emphasizes the role of AQUAS in practice (Sect. 6.3).

References

1. Xu, C., Xia, F., Sharaf, M.A., Zhou, M., Zhou, A.: AQUAS: a quality-aware scheduler for NoSQL data stores. In: ICDE, pp. 1210–1213 (2014)
2. Cooper, B.F., Silberstein, A., Tam, E., Ramakrishnan, R., Sears, R.: Benchmarking cloud serving systems with YCSB. In: SoCC, pp. 143–154 (2010)
3. Chi, Y., Jin Moon, H., Hacigümüs, H.: ICBS: Incremental cost-based scheduling under piecewise linear SLAs. PVLDB 4(9), 563–574 (2011)
4. Labrinidis, A., Roussopoulos, N.: Exploring the tradeoff between performance and data freshness in database-driven web servers. VLDB J. 13(3), 240–255 (2004)
5. Ahmad, M., Aboulnaga, A., Babu, S., Munagala, K.: Interaction-aware scheduling of report-generation workloads. VLDB J. 20(4), 589–615 (2011)
6. Ahmad, M., Duan, S., Aboulnaga, A., Babu, S.: Predicting completion times of batch query workloads using interaction-aware models and simulation. In: EDBT, pp. 449–460 (2011)
7. Rabl, T., Sadoghi, M., Jacobsen, H.-A., Gómez-Villamor, S., Muntés-Mulero, V., Mankowskii, S.: Solving big data challenges for enterprise application performance management. PVLDB 5(12), 1724–1735 (2012)
8. Patil, S., Polte, M., Ren, K., Tantisiriroj, W., Xiao, L., López, J., Gibson, G., Fuchs, A., Rinaldi, B.: YCSB++: benchmarking and performance debugging advanced features in scalable table stores. In: SoCC, p. 9 (2011)
9. Xu, C., Sharaf, M.A., Zhou, X., Zhou, A.: Quality-aware schedulers for weak consistency key-value data stores. Distrib. Parallel Databases 32(4), 535–581 (2014)

Chapter 7
Conclusion and Future Work

Abstract The chapters above clearly present the problem of quality-aware scheduling in key-value data stores as well as the related literature and researches, the scheduling strategies for both state-transfer and operation-transfer updates, and a prototype of quality-aware scheduler as well as a typical web application. In this chapter, we briefly summarize the research of this book and discuss the future work according to the limitations in study and the application-driven demand. In the following, Sect. 7.1 concludes our work of this book; Sect. 7.2 discusses some related open issues.

Keywords Core Issue · Summary · Future Work

7.1 Conclusion

Data consistency simplifies to the freshness of data accessed by queries at a local node. Clearly, the latency/consistency trade-off at node level further boils down to finding the trade-off between query latency (i.e., quality of service (QoS)) and data freshness (i.e., quality of data QoD)). In real application, different web queries or users would have different expectations in terms of QoS and QoD. In this work, the core issue is to optimize QoS and QoD at node level and the detailed research is listed as follows:

- *The general asynchronous update model in distributed key-value stores as well as the metrics of QoS and QoD are analyzed, in order to formally define the quality-aware scheduling problem.* With the help of analysis on the data structure model, data replication as well as the consistency, user query and system update in key-value stores, the components strongly related to quality-aware scheduling are abstracted and modeled in this work. Meanwhile, service-level agreement and freshness-level agreement are adopted to measure QoS and QoD, respectively. Based on that, the quality-aware scheduling problem is formally defined in distributed key-value stores.
- *Freshness/Tardiness, Adaptive Freshness/Tardiness mechanisms, as well as the popularity-aware versions are designed, which efficiently support quality-aware*

© The Author(s) 2015   95
C. Xu and A. Zhou, *Quality-aware Scheduling for Key-value Data Stores*,
SpringerBriefs in Computer Science, DOI 10.1007/978-3-662-47306-1_7

scheduling for state-transfer updates. Toward the key-value stores with state-transfer updates, freshness/tardiness (FIT) is employed to consider the requirement on both QoS and QoD by selectively installing updates, i.e., applying or skipping updates. In order to explore deadlines to further balance, the trade-off between QoS and QoD, the variant of FIT, i.e., adaptive freshness/tardiness (AFIT), is adopted in this work. In addition, popularity is leveraged to address skewed data access pattern under popularity-aware mechanism. This mechanism groups the queries access the same data object into a query group as the scheduling unit. Hence, a suite of approaches efficiently support quality-aware scheduling for state-transfer updates.

- *The approximate algorithms for freshness/tardiness mechanism and popularity-aware version are proposed, which reduce the computational complexity of quality-aware scheduling for operation-transfer updates.* Freshness/tardiness mechanism is extended toward the key-value stores with operation-transfer updates. The decision in FIT for operation-transfer updates goes beyond a simple binary decision of installing or skipping updates to a more general case of deciding how many updates to install, although the principles are the same with the one for state-transfer updates. Similarly, the decision in popularity-aware FIT for operation-transfer updates goes beyond the binary decision to the more general case. Hence, in order to reduce the cost on computing the number of updates under frequent updates, we propose approximate algorithms which reduce the computational complexity of quality-aware scheduling for operation-transfer updates.

- *The prototype of quality-aware scheduler as well as its benchmark is implemented, on which an online application supported by quality-aware scheduling is demonstrated.* By exploring the technique details of implementation on distributed key-value stores, the prototype framework of a quality-aware scheduler is depicted and a prototype system based on Cassandra, namely AQUAS, is implemented in this work. In addition, a benchmark for quality-aware scheduling in distributed key-value stores, as well as the implementation of QCSB benchmark based on YCSB, is illustrated here. As an example, a timeline query on microblog is demonstrated on AQUAS in order to show how to support online applications. Hence, both the prototype framework and the benchmark for this quality-aware scheduler as well as the high-level online applications are provided as a complete and valid solution.

In summary, this study focuses on quality-aware scheduling in key-value stores, designs a prototype framework of quality-aware scheduler, and illustrates the scheduling supports online applications. This research with its coherence and sustainablity forms a relatively complete component in itself. This work is based on the comprehensive survey and analysis of state-of-the-art theories and techniques. The theory analysis as well as extensive experiments show that the proposed solutions for quality-aware scheduling achieve significant efficiency and effectiveness.

7.2 Future Work

In this work, we start-off by the core issue of optimizing QoS and QoD at node level, and derive a series of issues, such as the scheduling toward different asynchronous update and how to support online applications, as well as the solutions. However, this work still leaves room for improvement and the future work can be considered from the following aspects.

- *Scheduling toward complex QoS and QoD penalties.* Here, QoS and QoD penalties are measured by piecewise linear functions which is appropriate in many application scenarios [1]. However, the semantic of piecewise linear functions might not be enough to specify users' expectation on QoS and QoD in some cases. The future work could extend them to be nonlinear functions and improve the scheduling strategies in this case.
- *The lighter approach for cost estimator.* The AQUAS prototype is implemented in Cassandra. In particular, the cost estimator adopts the approach based on historical statistics which is relatively simple. Although the overhead of this approach is acceptable, the future work might adopt the other methods to further reduce the overhead. These works [2–5] are related to this topic.
- *Various kinds of online applications.* In this study, we take a microblogging system as an example to illustrate quality-aware scheduling based on AQUAS. However, there are many other scenarios which call for quality-aware scheduling. The future work could implement more applications and further highlight the various applications based on AQUAS in practice.

References

1. Chi, Y., Moon, H.J., Hacigümüs, H.: ICBS: incremental cost-based scheduling under piecewise linear SLAs. PVLDB **4**(9), 563–574 (2011)
2. Ahmad, M., Duan, S., Aboulnaga, A., Babu, S.: Predicting completion times of batch query workloads using interaction-aware models and simulation. In: EDBT, pp. 449–460 (2011)
3. Wu, W., Chi, Y., Hacigümüs, H., Naughton, J.F.: Towards predicting query execution time for concurrent and dynamic database workloads. PVLDB **6**(10), 925–936 (2013)
4. Wu, W., Chi, Y., Zhu, S., Tatemura, J., Hacigümüs, H., Naughton, J.F.: Predicting query execution time: are optimizer cost models really unusable? In: ICDE, pp. 1081–1092 (2013)
5. Wu, W., Wu, X., Hacigümüs, H., Naughton, J.F.: Uncertainty aware query execution time prediction. PVLDB **7**(14), 1857–1868 (2014)

Printed in the United States
By Bookmasters